I ONCE KNEW EVERYTHING

JAMES AGEE JR.

ALSO BY JAMES AGEE JR.

Books

- Jim
- Bontrix
- Under The Mountains
- Mask City
- NReluctant Words
- Salem's Wake
- Octoshi
- Scatter Scratch
- Dead of Night
- Cajun Dusk
- Moonrise Souls
- Nightfall Empire
- A Mountain Among Many

∽

Anthologies

- Once Upon A Spell
- Tales of Red

- Something Wicked
- Nightmares Live Here
- Neon Lights
- Never After
- Lessons Learned
- Misunderstood

I Once Knew Everything © 2021 James Agee Jr.

All rights reserved under the International and Pan-American Copyright Conventions. No part of this book may be reproduced or transmitted in any form or by any means, electronic or mechanical, including photocopying, recording, or by any information storage and retrieval system, without the permission in writing from the publisher.

The unauthorized reproduction or distribution of this copyrighted work is illegal. Criminal copyright infringement, including infringement without monetary gain, is investigated by the FBI and is punishable by up to 5 years in prison and a fine of $250,000.

Editor: Katie Johns

PREFACE

There was a time in my life when I thought that I knew everything. Over the years, as I grew into being an adult I seemed to have less epiphanies about life and focus more on being a proper member of society. I told you that I once knew everything, and that is true, but what I didn't mention is that I was a child when I knew everything.

If you think that I am making this up, simply ask anyone in my family. You could pose a question to me when I was a child and I would respond in my broken child English by saying something intelligible but lengthy in response. At this point I would be asked, "How do you know that?" I would respond matter-of-factly, "I know ehh-bee-stang."

I am not writing this to expand on my knowledge as a child, I am writing this because as I grow older, I find that I am forgetting some of the little moments that helped make me into the person that I am today. You see, it is those small everyday moments that I believe we long for the most once we have left childhood behind. This is simply my way of preserving some of mine as I remember them.

Effort has been made to protect the anonymity of the people in these stories. My close friends and family will have no trouble deciphering the people in these tales. In order for me to tell these stories of mine with as much factual reverence as possible, I felt it necessary to leave out some names. These are the stories, my stories, of the things that have happened in my life. This is perhaps one of the most difficult things that I will ever write, but I believe that it is important to preserve as many memories as possible.

These are the stories of my struggles and triumphs, of my good days and bad, of the times when I thought that I was having a regular day that turned out to be something special, and of all of the moments in-between. I wish that I could remember more stories from my past, but I am thankful to have been able to hold onto the ones that I have. Remembering is a gift that can sometimes heal and other times it can hurt, but it is a gift that should be cherished.

One truth that I would always say as a child was, "People are people, and people can do what they want to do." I think about that sometimes. It is a bold statement, even for a child to make. Yet, there is so much truth in the first part. "People are people." I would say, because I knew it to be true. Most of the stories in this book would not have happened had it not been for the people in my life.

Join me on this journey as we attempt to understand that people are people, and try to discover a time in our lives when perhaps we all knew everything.

1

ALIVE

I was born July 24, 1993. Shortly thereafter I fell sick and was taken back to the hospital. I was diagnosed with Group B Strep. I had a rough time fighting it and the doctors were not entirely sure that I would make it. In infants and children Group B Strep can be deadly.

God had a plan for me because I did make it through and am here writing this book. It was a fight for my life that I cannot recount with vivid detail because I was too young to recall. I cannot begin to imagine what my parents must have been feeling. I was their first child and they were excited to have me join their family, and then unexpectedly they were told that I might not survive. The uncertainty of all of the problems that life can throw at a person must make being a new parent one of the most stressful experiences imaginable.

It has always been a practice of mine to be thankful for each and every day. It is a blessing just to be alive. There is no guarantee that today won't be terrible or that it won't be magnificent, but the fact that you are alive right now and able to experience the joy and sadness of living is a wonder all its own. Every day I thank God for the chance to be alive. If it is raining outside, I thank him for the rain. If it is a sunny day, then I thank him for the sun and nice weather. I see everything as God's creation and when you start to view things through that lens you are able to appreciate every little aspect of your day.

In my life thus far, I have experienced great joy along with great sadness. I would prefer the moments of joy, but I am thankful to have been here to experience the sadness too. All emotions are a part of being alive and human. Sometimes I wonder if I think about things too much, but it is in that time spent wondering that I have learned to see the beauty in everything around me. Trust me, it's there if you only make the effort of looking. If you are reading this, then you are alive and that means you have been given a gift. Perhaps it is only the gift of this moment, but it is yours and yours alone to appreciate.

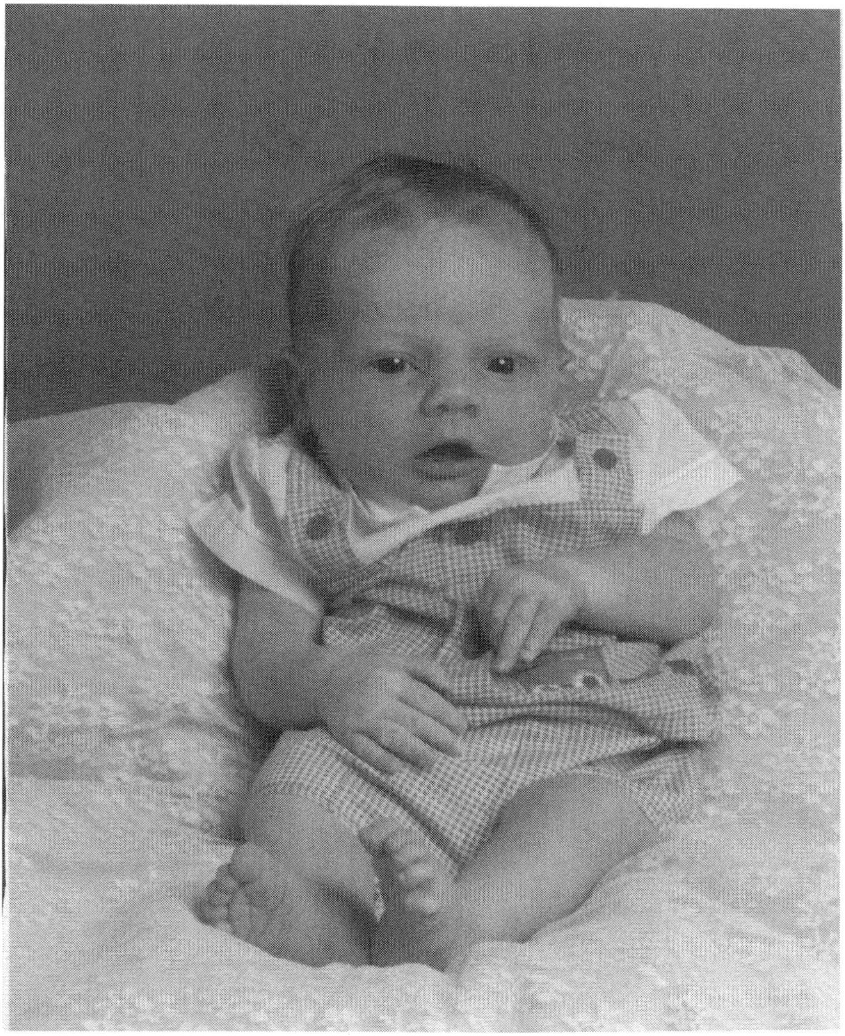

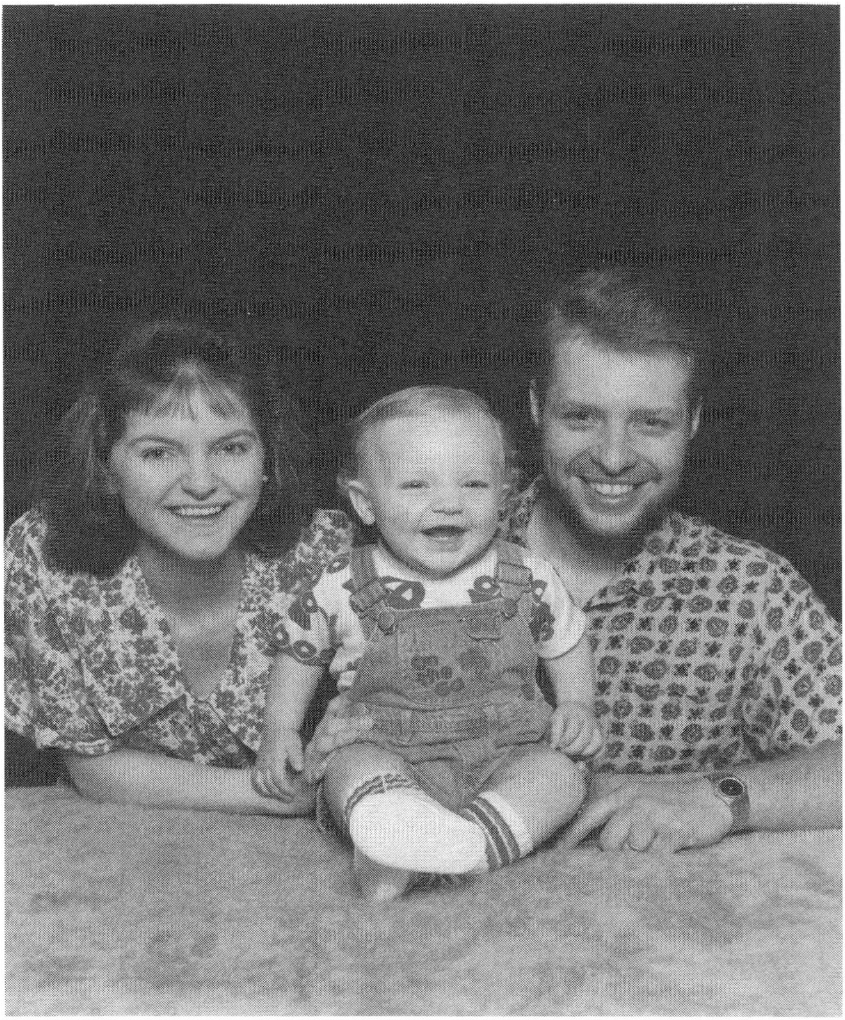

2

I LOVE YOU

Growing up, I had what I consider to be a happy childhood. There were constants in my life and that has always been something that I thrive on. I have so many fond memories of my elementary school days. Most days would start with a similar routine of being driven to school by my Aunt Diane and my Mom, Sheila. Over the years the vehicle might have changed, but the people driving it seldom ever did.

School was an exciting place to go each day. It was the place with all of the new technology. They had brand new Windows computers that were in color and there was one game in particular that I looked forward to playing. I cannot remember the title of the game, but the main character was a bee and your goal was to type the correct letters and words to help it navigate the hive.

Before being introduced to the amazing wonders of

Kindergarten and school in the 90's, I had to go through the basics. Preschool didn't work for me, so I just cried nonstop for the first few days until my parents agreed that I would just have to skip it and learn at home for that year, so my first experience with actual school was when I started Kindergarten.

My cousin, Jeremiah, and I were inseparable, so the teachers decided that it would be best to place us in different classes. To this day, I still don't understand the logic behind that. My entire time in elementary school, the teachers made it their goal to separate the two of us. It was as if they thought that having two relatives in the same class would be harmful to our social development. Actually, that is exactly what they thought.

Regardless, it didn't work. We still found plenty of times throughout the day where we could talk and disrupt their plans of separating the two of us. Since we were in the same grade throughout school, it worked out that my Aunt and Mom would take us to school each morning. We would stand at this giant glass window that stretched from floor to ceiling and before the school day would begin, the two of them would sign "I Love You" to the two of us. It wasn't actual sign language because it was simple enough that a Kindergartner could easily understand it. They would point to themselves, "I." Then they would cross their chests with their arms, like and X, "Love". Finally, they would point towards us, "You". All together it was a "secret" message from them to us.

I miss how simple those days were. It was a simple

routine to look forward to, but it is one that I have always remembered. Something else that I have a hard time forgetting is the time that I threw up on the way to school. My Aunt was driving, my Mom in the passenger seat, and I told them that I wasn't feeling good. My Aunt told me if I needed to throw up not to worry about the car, just roll the window down and do what I needed to do. I rolled the window down and threw up all over the side of her car.

My Aunt has since passed away, but it is the little moments like those that I remember. She loved her vehicles and was always proud when she would get a new one, so to not even care about me getting sick all over one says a lot about her. She always had a tough exterior that a lot of people saw, but I knew her and I knew the truth. She loved her family.

Many things have changed since then, but one thing is still the same. "I Love You".

3

SKELETON IN THE CABINET

I recall very little about my first-grade year of school, other than a specific event that occurred the first week of classes. The classroom that I would be in for the remainder of the year was a very dull brown color, embellished with bland grays and other muted tones. I have never understood why schools and prisons tend to have similar color schemes, but that was the case then and tends to be the case now.

The way that my elementary school was set up made it so that these very large rooms were divided into separate classrooms using storage cabinets. I know this sounds like an odd setup, and truthfully looking back on it, I think it was. You could easily hear the lessons that were taking place in the class beside of yours. If you were lucky the nearest class would be learning something really interesting and you could listen in on what was happening there instead of paying attention to what was being taught in your class. Sometimes, a student would do something so terrible that the teacher would yell at them so loudly that the other teachers in the room would have to stop their lessons until the shouting was over.

All of that was strange enough, but that is not what I remember about my first-grade class. During the first week of school my classroom teacher wanted to establish ground rules and make it clear that she would not tolerate any misbehavior. This did not upset me because I never acted out in class or caused disruptions to begin with. She walked slowly around the classroom, eyeing each of us and making us feel like we had done something wrong.

"In this class we do not tolerate breaking the rules."

I wondered what classes did tolerate rule breaking.

"It is highly recommended that you follow the rules and do as you are told."

She rushed over to one of the cabinets that separated our class from the one beside of us. The cabinet had a wood paneled front and horrendous orange sides, clearly an original from when the school had been built. She pulled open the cabinet, the magnetic closure making a distinctly metal sound as she did. Her eyes were wild with the knowing that whatever she would say next was going to come as a shock to the class.

There was nothing inside of the cabinet, except for a skeleton. This was the first skeleton that I had ever seen in a classroom, in fact it was the first skeleton that I had ever seen in person.

"Do you know what this is?" She asked, a malevolent grin spread across her face.

She paused and waited for one of us to raise our hand and answer. None of us did, we were too afraid of her to speak.

"This was one of my previous students. They didn't follow the rules, so I locked them inside of this cabinet and left them."

She stood there, cabinet door open, for a few moments longer to allow us to get a good look at the skeleton in the closet. After a minute or two she closed the cabinet, making sure that the magnetic clasp had clicked into place and that it was shut properly.

"Now, we're going to follow the rules this year, aren't we? We don't want to end up like the student in the cabinet, do we?"

I don't believe that she truly expected any of us to answer. That was the beginning of a school year that I have almost completely blocked from my memory. It's strange because I have such vivid memories of my other school years, even the content that we learned those years, but for first grade the only thing that I can recall with certainty are the dour colors of the room and remnants of a disobedient child locked in the cabinet.

4
100%

If you grew up in the 90's you know what a Tamagotchi is. For everyone else, they were portable games that were extremely popular. The point was to raise a "creature" of some type from the time that it hatches as an egg until it dies. Yes, a children's game where the goal is to raise something until it dies. Sometimes I long for the unpredictability of the 90's. This was not so unusual in a time where you could casually buy purple or green ketchup at your local Wal-Mart.

I had owned one of the keychain versions where there are really only a few buttons to press to complete tasks within the game. One day while looking at the toy store at the mall--yes we had actual toy stores back then--I saw a Tamagotchi Gameboy Color game. As with most games of the time, it had the potential to be terrible, but I wanted it anyway.

Since the only way to get anything that I wanted back

then was to beg my parents for it, I told them that I wanted that game. They agreed that they would get it for me if I passed my spelling test that was coming up at the end of the week.

"No problem!" I thought to myself, ignoring the fact that I always missed at least one question on those tests. After all, if I didn't pass I just wouldn't get the game. Not passing was not an option. The day of the test came and we had a substitute teacher. This was unusual because we normally never had a substitute teacher on a day when we would be having a test. For some reason, as a second grader, I thought that teachers really planned their sick days and that it had to align perfectly with their lesson plans. They couldn't get sick if there was going to be a test tomorrow. Years later, now that I am a teacher myself, I see that I was correct.

I took my time writing down the letters to make the words as the substitute teacher called them out to us. One habit that I had back then was going back and second-guessing myself. Luckily, I got to a point in my life where I stopped going back to change my answers. Now if I think something is incorrect, I just say, "Oh well," and move on. I would like to say that about an hour later when I got my spelling test back it had a "100%" written on the top of it, but that isn't what happened.

When I got my paper back, it didn't have anything written on it. The substitute called us each up to the teacher's desk one-by-one to tell us our grades. For some strange reason, she thought that just telling us our grades would be enough. If I remember correctly, there was one response on mine that had a red "X" beside of it. So, I had the paper and no grade on the top. It occurred to me that I could still get my 100% and Tamagotchi game.

I went back to my seat and asked the girl next to me if I could borrow her red ink pen. She was the type of student that brought an entire office's worth of stationary with her to class, the kid that you just knew would materialize a massive set of Crayola's come time for art class. She handed me the ink pen and didn't think much about it until she saw me write a 100% on the top of my paper.

"I should tell on you." She said, her smug teacher's pet smile spread across her face.

"We're friends though. Don't say anything." I said.

I was not a devious child, and the reason that this stands out in my mind so much is because I never cheated either. This was the first time that I had ever thought to do anything like that before.

"Fine. Give me my ink pen back." She said, jerking the pen from my hand.

Later that evening when I showed off the paper with the "100%" written at the top my parents were excited for me. They had anticipated that I would get all of the spelling words correct because we had studied them so many times. They handed me the game and I smiled, happy to have gotten what I wanted.

"Hmm. That's odd." My Dad said.

"What?" Mom said concernedly.

I knew exactly what they were looking at. That substitute teacher had to go and write an "X" on that one question.

"How did you get a 100% if you missed one?" My Mom asked.

"I don't know. We had a substitute today and she must have made a mistake. See at the top, it has a 100% on it." I said, never having been a good liar.

"Ok, then just take it back to class tomorrow and make sure with your regular teacher." Mom said.

I knew that they had caught me in my lie. They were not going to let me get away with it so easily. So the next day I took the paper back to school and was crazy enough to ask my regular teacher to write a 100% on the top of it in her handwriting because my parent's didn't believe me. She was about to do it too when the teacher's pet raised her hand. I say that she raised her hand but it was more like an enthusiastic wave.

"Teacher! Teacher! He didn't make a 100%! He missed one and used my ink pen to cheat!"

I wanted to be mad at her, but I honestly should have saw that one coming. At the end of the day, that student's loyalties were with my teacher and nobody else.

"Is this true?" My teacher asked me.

"Yes." I said quietly. My insides were like ice and I couldn't have felt more guilty than if I had just been convicted with a crime.

"This is so unlike you." She said.

I don't remember what kind of punishment I received

after that, or if there was one at all, but I do remember the terrible feeling of having disappointed my teacher and my parents. I have always been someone that values education and respecting my elders, so not only did it feel like a betrayal of my teacher and parents, but it felt like I had betrayed myself.

One lesson that I learned was to never borrow a red ink-pen from the teacher's pet; they will be too suspicious and there is no way that you are going to get away with whatever it is you needed the pen for in the first place.

5
A PINCH OF SPIT

School lunches have never been something that I looked forward to. In fact, throughout elementary and high school I rarely ate them, preferring either to go without or to bring something from home that I actually liked. I believe that this all stemmed from an incident when I was in the second grade.

My class had about twenty students in it and I knew pretty much all of them. One of the students really wanted to be mine and my cousin's friend. I learned that being friends with someone meant that you would have to eat lunch with them, play with them on the playground at recess, and other things that friends did.

My cousin and I had always been close, growing up together and being the same age, so we had a lot in common and it didn't seem like work being friends with him. However, being friends with the other kids in class took a lot of effort. It wasn't because I was unable to be nice to them, I have never had an issue with being kind to others, but it was because we were just so different.

Other kids liked doing thing that most children enjoyed doing. My cousin and I did things that kids do, but our interests just didn't align with theirs. Even in the second grade I was more interested in making up stories and working on anything creative that I could get my hands on, whereas my classmates were overjoyed to be able to play "school" during recess.

I'm not kidding when I say that one of my classmates favorite games to play was pretending to have class at recess. The whole point in recess is to take a break. I would spend a lot of my break time playing board games or tag, which was another popular option. However, recess aside, none of these kids were anyone that I would want to hang out with after school ended.

One of the kids that I was "friends" with would sit with my cousin and I at lunch. He was friendly, but loved to talk and when he talked he would often spit and food would go flying along with it. It was very common to be eating lunch next to him or somewhere nearby and feel the spray of spit as he launched into a discussion of how awesome recess was that day.

There were times when his food would miraculously land on my tray due to it flying from his mouth and landing there. It got to the point where I couldn't bring myself to eat lunch anymore. It didn't help that we were seated alphabetically at lunch. Some students would find ways of sitting near their friends by switching seats when the teacher wasn't looking, but I didn't stand a chance. This kid wanted to be my friend and his last name started with the letter "B". My last name being "Agee", I was always first when it came to alphabetical order.

Luckily my cousin's last name started with a "B" too, so he always sat nearby. Sometimes, when the school tried to separate us into different classes he would be placed at a different table, but the majority of the time we were able to have lunch together.

When I told my parents that I wasn't eating the school lunches because a kid was spitting on them they called the principal. The next day the principal called me to his office to ask what was going on.

"This is highly unlike him to do something like this." He said to me.

I sat there and couldn't speak. I had never been called to the principal's office before and I respected school so much that it felt like the end of the world to me. I tried to speak, but I simply couldn't bring myself to.

"Okay, if you won't tell me what's going on then there isn't much that I can do." He finally relented after ten minutes of trying to get me to talk.

The teacher did separate us at lunch, but after that I had lost my appetite for school lunches. I know it sounds crazy, but I believe that when things like that happen to us as children it can sometimes stick with us throughout adulthood. I did end up being friends with that kid at school, but I just couldn't eat lunch near him. In high school, I brought a bag of Cheeze-It crackers with me for lunch each day. Lunch ended up being a time when I could get my homework done so that I wouldn't have to do it at home.

On days when the school served pepperoni-cheese rolls, a favorite of the students and staff, I would get in line and get one just so that I could sell it to the highest bidder. Often times I would sell a single lunch for $5 just because it was pepperoni-cheese roll day. It was even better when they called for extras because I could double my money.

That same year in second grade, there was a girl that didn't seem to have any friends. I wondered why nobody wanted to play with her at recess or be her friend, but I quickly learned the reason. This girl would crawl under a large table at the entrance to the classroom and hide there until someone would enter. As you walked by she would reach out and grab your leg and start pinching it. She thought that it was hilarious and would cackle from underneath the table.

The teacher had apparently tried everything that she could with that student, because eventually she told us all not to go around her because she was afraid that she would pinch us. The administration did step in and that student had to attend behavioral based pull-out classes, though she was still in our classroom most of the day.

Friends in school are such a big part of the experience. I guess that I just never felt like I needed a big group of friends if I had one or two that I liked being around. The same goes for when I was in high school. I had a few good friends and though I was friendly with all of my classmates, I was never in any particular group. I guess that you could say everyone was my friend, but my best friends were the ones that I would choose to spend my time with. If you have a few good friends then you truly don't need a million others.

6
DINOSAUR EGG

I had quite a few toys when I was younger. My parents would get my brother and I action figures pretty regularly. There was a K.B. Toy store in our mall and we loved going inside and walking the narrow isles jam-packed with toys. The adults who worked at the store loved talking about the products that they sold so much that I remember telling my parents that I wanted to work at a toy store when I grew up. I am very thankful that I do not work at a toy store because I have always believed you should have a passion for the products that you sell and I simply don't have a passion for action figures.

There was another store in the mall that we went to frequently and would buy toys at. I remember the name of this store because I thought it was funny that it sounded so much like my own name. The store was called Ames. Think about it, it is just the name "James" without the "J". They would carry a random selection of toys and on more than one occasion I remember getting something from there.

It was always either my parents or Nanny and Papaw that would buy me toys from Ames. We were eating at K&W Cafeteria, a restaurant in the mall, and I had gotten my usual favorite dessert of strawberry shortcake. The strawberry shortcake from K&W was always mine and my Papaw's favorite dessert from there. The only thing that could make the trip to the mall better would be if I got a new toy, so we went to Ames on the search for just that. My Mom was with us and she was very used to me asking for things when we would go to the store, but I knew if she said, "No." that my Papaw would more than likely say, "Yes."

It didn't take me long to find something that I wanted. My brother had found a toy that he wanted, but instead of just one thing, I decided that I wanted two! They had a small selection of "Science" toys in that department and I discovered a red handheld microscope. It looked like a tiny red tube and you could hold it over something while looking through it to get a magnified view. It was about the same shape and size as an ink pen, only slightly rounder in circumference.

I had no intention of using it as a microscope, rather I thought it looked like a good substitute for a magic wand and wanted it for that purpose. I would always use toys for some other purpose than they were intended, imagining the many different ways that it could fit into my fictional world. The second item that I found and wanted as a Magic 8 Ball.

If you have never seen a Magic 8 Ball before then you are sadly missing out. They look like giant black billiard balls with the number eight painted on the top in white. You would shake the ball while asking a question and it would present to you an answer when you turned it over. I was mesmerized by how unpredictable this item was. You could ask a question but until you stopped shaking it, you never knew what the answer would be. I had to have it!

Mom told me that I didn't need either of them, but my plan to ask my Papaw to buy them for me was a success. I recall getting hours of enjoyment from both of those products that were not technically toys, but that I used as such.

On one of our weekend trips to Beckley, West Virginia to shop, we went to Toys-R-Us. I remember thinking that it was possibly the biggest and best toy store in the world. K.B. Toys was good, but Toys-R-Us was great. They had a much larger selection than our toy store at the local mall. I found so many things that I wanted, but one item in particular stood out from the rest.

They were selling Jurassic Park Dinosaur Eggs that would hatch and have a dinosaur inside. I thought that my only opportunity to own a real living dinosaur was right before me. If my parents didn't get it for me, then I would regret that for the rest of my life. There was a desperate urgency to my pleas for the dinosaur egg. I knew that if my parents would just buy me one then I would be able to take really good care of it.

My dinosaur would not grow up to be one of the mean

ones that ate people. No, I would raise it to be gentle and kind. The type of dinosaur that you could take on walks at the park and offer food to without worrying that it would bite off your fingers. Instead I envisioned my dinosaur slowly nibbling on the food in my hand.

I ended up getting the dinosaur egg and when I got it home I hatched the dinosaur. It was a really cool toy, but like most toys of that time period, it didn't live up to my expectations. I was fortunate then to have an extremely overactive imagination, something that I think is great for children and adults alike, so I was able to really enjoy the toy, regardless of the fact that it wasn't a living and breathing dinosaur like I had wanted.

I should have known better than to think that you could purchase a live dinosaur at Toys-R-Us, or that my parents would even allow me to have a living dinosaur at that age. As an adult, I realize that my assumptions as a child were often times incorrect. After all, everyone knows that in order to get a real dinosaur, you have to travel to Jurassic Park.

7

BUTTER BREAD

I have never considered myself to be super healthy. I make semi-healthy food choices now, but as a child, I never put much consideration into the types of foods that I consumed. As far as I was concerned, candy was a part of the food pyramid and made for a great meal substitution. No, my parents never fed me candy instead of dinner, I always had a hot meal, but my mindset was that I could eat absolutely anything that I wanted and be okay.

One of my favorite unhealthy snacks as a child was butter bread or peanut butter and sugar on bread. My Nanny was the one who used to serve me a piece of bread with butter on it. I loved everything about it. It was a simple recipe that I could make any time on my own and it tasted amazing. Looking back, that was probably not the healthiest choice for a snack, but it didn't stop me from walking to their house and asking for it anyway.

We lived nearby, so it was a very short walk from my house to theirs. At least there was some exercise involved in getting from one place to another. Nowadays, I would not dream of eating a slide of bread with butter on it. I actually don't like the idea of butter at all. Since learning of how unhealthy butter is, I try and avoid it in all of the meals that I cook.

It was just something that I enjoyed as a kid. Not knowing how bad it was for me was part of what made it so appetizing. I don't remember worrying about how many calories or how much cholesterol was in the butter, but I remember the comfortable atmosphere of my Nanny and Papaw's home and the sense that I was always welcome. Though I still struggle to not eat an entire box of candy at a time, I no longer crave the taste of butter on bread, though I will forever remember those days as something special.

8
11:11

"It's 11:11, that's the biggest time on the clock!" My brother would say.

Every night before bed, sometimes even when we were already in bed, my brother would tell my parents and I that it was 11:11 and that it was the biggest time on the clock. When my parents asked him what he meant by that, he would just say, "It's the biggest time on the clock."

I have heard of people making wishes at 11:11, but this was something else entirely. My brother was convinced that somehow 11:11 was the biggest time that there could be. It didn't make sense to us, but it made sense to him, so it became something he would say every night.

I had little phrases that I would say at bedtime too. My go-to was, "Good night. Sleep tight. Don't let the beddy bugs bite." Ironically enough, I would the one with issues of spiders being in my bed later on. These just became the things that we would say at night time.

Now that I am older and live in a house by myself, I tell my dog goodnight. Sometimes I do it in French or Japanese, any language that I am trying to learn at the time. Oddly, my dog loves it when I speak French to her as she seems to respond better to it than English.

It's the little things like the way we said goodnight that I remember. Though it makes little to no sense, 11:11 will always be the biggest time on the clock in my mind, and I will always remember my little brother telling that to us with unwavering certainty.

9

T.V. LAND

For years I remember my Dad having a work schedule that wasn't great. At one point in time, his schedule required him to go to work at around 2 or 3 PM and return home late at night. He has worked as a machinist pretty much his entire adult life and is extremely skilled in what he does, but his work schedule has not always been very good.

During that time, I remember watching cartoon episodes of Spider Man and reruns of Bonanza with him before he would have to leave for work. My brother and I always hated it when he would have to leave because we wanted him to stay home all day. There was always a sense of excitement when he would come home at night, and more often than not we would stay up late so that we were awake to greet him when he got home.

In the evenings, we would start watching episodes of The

Brady Bunch, The Facts of Life, and Gilligan's Island with my mom. I loved those shows because something interesting was always happening in them. There was never an episode where they did nothing and sat around talking, there was always some conflict that could be resolved by the end of the show.

Though everything about The Brady Bunch was "outdated", I could not help but relate to some of the problems that the characters in the show faced. It seemed that each of these shows focused on issues that most people could relate to. The Facts of Life was so much different than anything else that I had seen on television, so I found it interesting too. There were a lot of older shows that I remember watching with my parents, but those three were regulars in the evenings while we waited for my Dad to return home from work.

Gilligan's Island was possibly my favorite because the setting was so exotic. I had never been to an island before and found the concept of being stranded on one to be exciting. The characters were all very unique from one another and somehow it all seemed to work. Years later, I would have the opportunity to meet and work with the main actor's wife. Bob Denver, known as Gilligan in the show, loved West Virginia and that is where his wife, Dreama Denver, currently resides. There is a radio station called Little Buddy Radio that exists in his honor.

One summer, I was working at a cultural festival held at a state park and she was there working too. She also hosted many local events that I attended, such as open mic nights at Gary Bowling's House of Art. She has always been a supporter of the arts and is selfless in her kindness towards West Virginia.

After watching a few episodes of those shows it would finally be time for Dad to walk through the front door. Some nights he would have surprises for us, like candy, but we didn't care so much about that because we just wanted him to be home.

One time, he brought us a candy that I still remember though I have not seen it since then. It was a small blue box that said "Rock Candy Crystals" on it. Inside were fragments of rock candy that resembled the look of actual crystals. They were pure sugar, and I loved every ounce of them.

Other shows that we would watch with my parents were: The Munsters, Happy Days, The Cosby Show, Bewitched, The Addams Family, Family Matters, Andy Griffith, The A-Team, Different Strokes, Full House, The Fresh Prince of Bel-air, Good Times, Growing Pains, Home Improvement, Boy Meets World, Laverne and Shirley, Leave It To Beaver, Little House on the Prairie, The Waltons, and pretty much anything that was from a previous time period. I loved all of those old shows because they weren't as hectic or difficult to relate to as more modern shows. I think that a lot of what is missing from television today is the heart that went into writing episodes about problems that real people face.

I don't know if it was that the shows were just that good or if I remember them as being amazing because of the time that I was spending with my parents. It might sound like I did nothing but watch television, which is simply not true, but the honest conversations that I had with my parents during that time and the experiences that we had through the lives of the characters on the T.V. screen, have formed some of my most precious memories. If given the choice, I would go back to the days where for a few hours each evening, while waiting for my family to all be together in one location, I could travel to a wonderful place called T.V. Land.

10

CHIPS AND COOKIES

My great grandmother on my mom's side of the family, known to me as Mawmaw, had a routine that I remember to this day. Whenever she would go get groceries, she would always bring my brother and I a pack of Richard Simmons Devil's Food Cake cookies and a can of Pringles each. This was something that she did for as long as I can remember.

She had to walk with a cane and her's was the metal-looking kind with the rubber stoppers on the bottom. I always looked forward to seeing her and the snacks that she would bring. Occasionally, she would mix things up and bring us Fudge Stripe Cookies, but it was always something that tasted great.

Eventually she got sick and was unable to go shopping for herself. When this happened, she still made sure that whoever was buying her groceries would pick up those cookies and chips for us. It was important to her because she knew how much my brother and I enjoyed it.

She was taken to a hospital in Roanoke, Virginia and things didn't look so good. My parents took my brother and I out of school for a few days so that we could go to the hospital and spend some time with her. I did not understand very much about what was happening, and I sure didn't grasp the concept of death, but when she passed away I felt a sorrow that I had never felt before. This was the first time that I recall experiencing the loss of someone close to me.

When I think of her, I still think of the evenings she would visit with us at my house, the pride that she had when she handed over the cookies and chips to us. Her eyes shining bright with happiness and joy. I wish that she had lived longer and that I had gotten to spend more time with her, getting to know her better. I will always carry with me the memories that I do have of her.

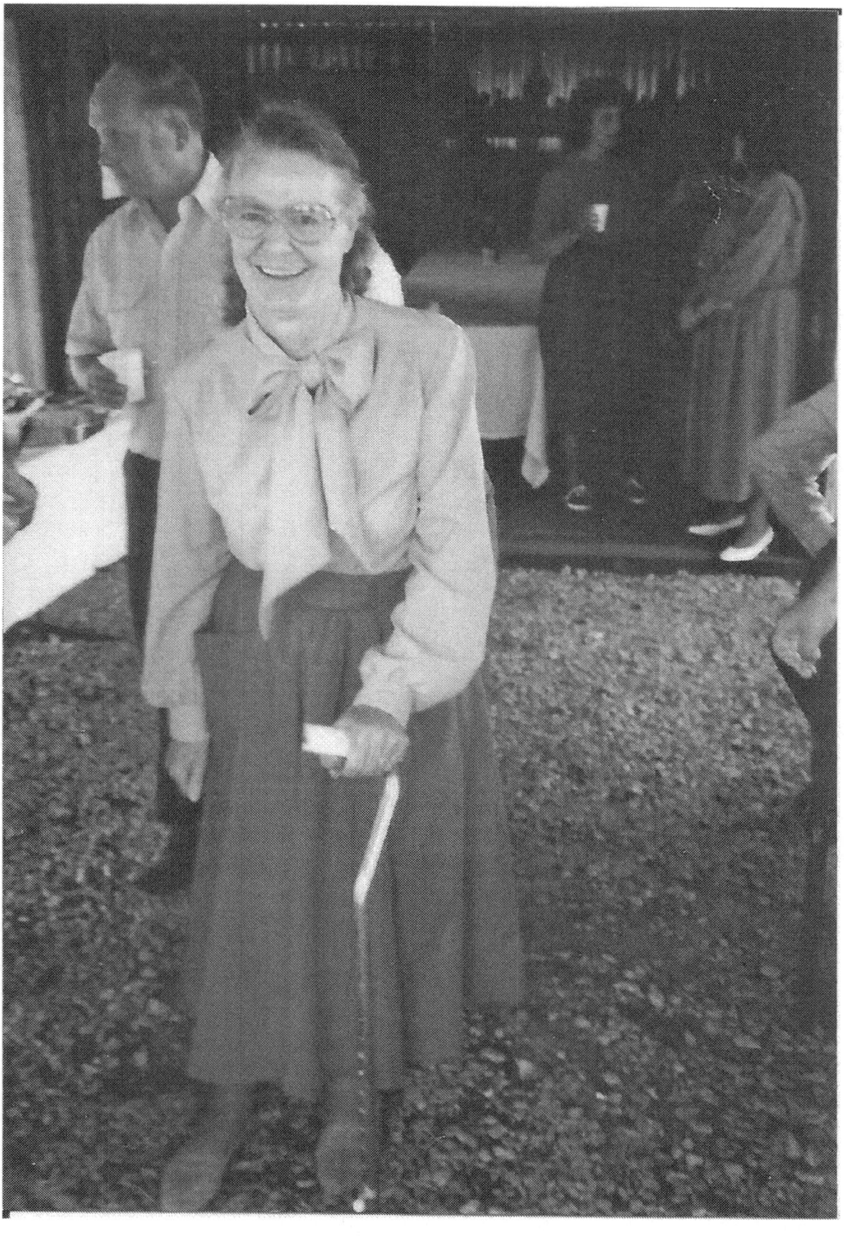

11

THE KELVINATOR

My great-grandparents on my Dad's side of the family were two very special people. I called them Grandma and Grandpa Thompson, on account of their last name being Thompson. Grandma Thompson had very light hair when I knew her, white but slightly blond. She would sit in a large recliner chair sipping on a jug sized bottle filled with ice water. Her health was not the best, but her personality shone through it.

Grandpa Thompson was a very quiet man. He never spoke much, but when he did you listened because you knew that he really had something to say. I was always impressed that he had been awarded the Purple Heart from his time serving in The Battle of the Bulge. When we would visit their house there would always be a tin can sitting on the table that he would spit his chewing tobacco into. I didn't think much of the habit at the time, not understanding tobacco and its health risks. I just thought that was part of who he was and that some people liked to chew on things and then spit them out.

They were both kind and loving individuals. Grandma was much more outspoken, and I think that she did most of the talking for the both of them. Sometimes we would watch whatever television show was playing in the background, but most of the time we would go there just to visit and talk with them. The linoleum flooring in the living room spread all the way to the kitchen, it was a brownish rock pattern that was not all that convincing.

"Go in the kitchen and get them something from the Kelvinator." Grandma Thompson would instruct my Dad.

Her weight did not allow her to move around very much, but she wanted to ensure that we were still comfortable and felt at home. It didn't take me long to realize that she was talking about the refrigerator when she said that. I later learned that there was once a brand of refrigerator called Kelvinator and she had just taken to calling it that.

Her fridge was full of diet soda drinks, never anything that was not diet, and I remember the first time I tried a diet soda was at their house. I also tried my first ever caramel apple sucker at their house. It is strange how food is so closely tied to our memories.

Grandpa Thompson had stomach troubles and therefore kept a very strict diet. You might think that he only ate foods without sodium or something like that, but his go-to meal was much stranger than anything I have ever witnessed anyone eat. He would take a piece of bread, put some bologna on top of it, a Swiss Roll Little Debbie cake on top of that, and then pour milk over the entire concoction. After mixing the combination together, his meal was prepared and ready to eat. I think that was just about the only combinations of foods that he liked eating.

Occasionally on visits Grandma Thompson would give my brother and I a few dollars to go buy a toy with. I wish that I had more time with them so that I could have gotten to know them even better, but the memories that I do have of them are some of the best that I can recall. Knowing that someone cares about you is one of the best gifts that anyone can give, and both of them gave that gift to me and my brother.

12

DISPOSABLE CAMERAS

Any time that there would be a field trip coming up at school or a vacation with my family, I would receive a disposable camera from my parents. I always loved getting those black and green FujiFilm cameras. There was something about having a camera, even one that would not remain mine after it was to be sent off for development, that made me feel like a grown-up.

As an adult I have a passion for photography and film cameras, but as a child I only saw it as something new and exciting. I didn't know the history of cameras and photography, though I did appreciate the art even then. I would bring home a permission slip from school telling of the exciting adventure that we would be going on as a class and my parents would say, "We will have to go to Sam's Club and get you a camera."

We almost always bought our disposable cameras from Sam's Club. They were also the place that developed film at the time, so our trip for the camera would begin and end there once it was time to send the film off. There was the thrill of knowing that I only had a certain number of photos that I could take and that if I wasn't careful, they might not turn out to look very good.

So often I would get back my photos from a trip and the flash would have been too bright and overexposed a photo so that little-to-nothing would be visible. I loved seeing the red-eye in the photos. It was always so much fun getting to see the people I knew with these strange red glowing spots coming from where their pupils should have been.

Now, I understand that there is a lot involved in taking a good photo with a film camera. I know that it is possible to get a good photo on every exposure. I also have come to learn the process for developing and scanning the photos after they have arrived at the photo lab. As a child, I just knew that I had a tiny rectangular box that would allow me to capture some of what I was seeing so that I could share it with my family later on.

I no longer have my photos developed, rather I opt to have them scanned and saved digitally. More than half of the photos that I take are now posted on social media to be viewed once and then forgotten. Gone are the days of flipping through a photo album and reminiscing over past events. I miss the thrill of waiting to see what my photos look like and then showing them to each person that I knew, taking the time to tell the accompanying stories as they flipped through each of the moments captured on photo-paper. Cameras and photography have been a big part of my life as an adult, and I cannot help but wonder if it all started with those plastic disposable cameras.

13
WINDOWS 95

When I think back on my addiction to technology, it is not hard for me to determine where it all started. It is not uncommon for a child nowadays to grow up with a tablet or computer at their disposal, but my childhood was not like that. I am actually very grateful that technology was not as popular when I was a child because I know that I would have spent my childhood in front of a glass screen rather than actually living.

It was my third-grade year, and aside from the treachery of having to learn multiplication, things were going pretty well. One day, my teacher walked into the classroom and said that she had some very big news to share with us.

I bet we will have to learn even more multiplication...I don't know if I can take any more of that.

"I will be holding a drawing to give away my old

computer because I bought a new one. I was thinking about it, and I know that not all of my students have a computer at home, so I thought that it would be nice to give it to one of you. Now, to be entered into the drawing you need to score an "A" on your tests and for each test that you score an "A" on, you will receive one entry." My teacher said, just as excited about this news as we all were.

Needless to say, I spent the next few weeks trying as hard as I possibly could to make "A's" on all of my tests. It was a strange feeling to be so excited about something that you didn't even know if you were going to win. I wasn't sure that winning a computer was something that could happen to me, I wasn't sure what kind of people won things, but I didn't figure that I was one of them.

I never considered myself to be unlucky, but I never considered myself to be lucky either. Luck was just something that people talked about, some intangible construct that a few people were graced with, but surely not a third-grade student like me.

The day arrived for her to draw a name for the computer. I looked around at my classmates and saw that they were all as excited and nervous as I was. The kid next to me was chewing on their fingernails with such ferocity that I worried they might bite their finger off.

This is it.

This is the moment that somebody wins a computer.

My teacher reached her had into the cardboard box that

held the tiny slips of paper with our names written on them. She pulled her hand out and had three slips of paper stuck together. She tossed two back into the box without having looked to see whose names were on them.

I bet that my name was on one of the slips of paper she threw back.

She took a deep breath, enjoying the suspenseful moment that she had created for her class, then said, "James Agee."

It was a very strange moment in time. I understand that I had not won a million dollars, but I believe that I experienced a moment that is similar to what someone who has won a million dollars would feel. I was numb for a moment that seemed to last an eternity and then it hit me all at once. An enormous smile spread across my face and though you might think the other third graders would be bitter about losing, they were congratulating me on winning.

"Do you want to go down to the office and call your parents to tell them that you won?" She asked.

I nodded my head, still in shock and unable to speak. This was really happening! I won a computer! It didn't matter to me that it was a Windows 95 computer, and it couldn't do much other than play a few pre-installed games and access dial-up internet. It also didn't occur to me that my parents would now have the expense of paying for dial-up internet if I were to use the enormous computer for anything more than multiplayer games of Mancala with my brother.

It was the idea of an entire world of possibility being available to me. Looking back on it, that was the start of my addiction to technology. Some part of me wonders what would have been different if I had not won that computer. I am grateful that my teacher, someone who was already underpaid and under appreciated, decided to give something of such value to a student in the pursuit of bettering their education. I have also wondered many times if she somehow knew that I would win because of how much I wanted it, though I am sure that I didn't want it any more than my classmates at the time did.

Had I not won that computer I know that technology would have infiltrated my life sooner or later. It was inevitable that I would end up spending so much of my time and career in front of a computer screen, but perhaps I would have had a few more years of being a child without a computer, the way that nature intended.

Technology opens up a world of possibility, that much is undisputed, but it also takes away certain aspects of life that I find myself longing for. No computer has ever been able to replicate the feeling of growing up in a world of true wonder, a world where you believe anything is possible only because you have never been told what is actually possible. I fear that computers offer us a world of possibility, but cloak the reality that true limitless imagination is hindered by the presentation of information on our screens.

By the time you read this, you may be using a hologram running on Windows 5,000 while floating around on your hoverboard, but one truth is bound to be evident and that is that there is nothing so exciting as the possibility of something that may or may not happen. Someday soon we may realize that technology is only a tool, not the center of possibility itself, but only if we are lucky...

14

PURPLE KETCHUP

Just about anyone who grew up in the ninteen-nineties can tell you about the crazy food options that we had. The nineties is responsible for some of the super unhealthy foods that can still be enjoyed to this day. While some of the unhealthy food remains, a lot of the crazy options that we had then are no longer available and have been discontinued. We had just about every flavor and variation of Sprite that you could imagine, Dunkaroos, any type of candy flavored cereal that you could dream of, and of course colored ketchup.

I have never really liked Ketchup very much, I prefer mustard, but there was no denying the appeal of colored ketchup. The colors that I remember being sold were red (of course), purple (a bright purple), green (yes, like grass), and blue (because why not). When I imagine colored ketchup, I think of very dull mixtures that still have strong undertones of red, but that was not the case. The colored ketchup of the nineties was bright and vibrant, just like all of the other ridiculous foods that were popular at the time. It is a mystery to me why they still don't offer the color options for ketchup as I am sure kids of any generation would enjoy it, but there is no doubt that the nineties spawned some of the most insane food ever created.

For the most part, my parents were willing to buy and try many of these crazy foods alongside my brother and I. If you don't believe that the food was as crazy as I say, just Google search Reese Swoops (candy shaped into the form of a potato chip). Perhaps my favorite of all of the lab-created foods was Torengos by Pringles. These were an extremely flavorful chip in the shape of a triangle. They had the perfect mixture of seasoning on them and it was not difficult to sit and eat an entire triangular shaped tube of them.

If I had a time machine and could go back to the nineties, I doubt that my main focus would be preserving the unhealthy foods of the time, but rather enjoying the common absurdity of it all. The more wild and unreal a product was, the better it seemed to sell. Brands and companies were not afraid to take risks and develop products that would possibly fail miserably. It is very obvious that companies now only try to develop what they think will be the most popular, not the most unique. Creativity was on full blast in the nineties and now it is secondary to profit margins. I don't know that the world will ever see a decade like the nineties, where impossible ideas were not only accepted but were celebrated. I was never a fan of the purple ketchup, or any of the colored ketchup for that matter, but I won't deny that I am glad it existed.

15

CRAZY FOR COFFEE

It is safe to say that children often mimic the adults around them. That is how we learn to be good citizens, by watching and repeating the things that we see those around us doing. When I was a child, I would look forward to my Nanny and Papaw visiting our house. We lived nearby and it was only a short walk for either of us to see one another.

Most days, I would see them at least once, and some evenings they would visit with my parents and stay for hours. Any time the baseball team, the Atlanta Braves, would be playing a game, my Papaw would be at our house watching it with my parents. I recall the hours of conversation that would accompany the games, never what the conversations were about but always the atmosphere of comfort. Perhaps that is why televised sports have always proven to be so popular, they allow a group of people to come together and form a community based on a common interest.

Aside from the conversations, there was always one other thing present and that was coffee. My parents would always make a fresh pot of coffee for the games, sometimes two or three pots depending on how much everyone was drinking. My Papaw can easily drink five or six cups of caffeinated coffee while I have only ever been lucky to manage one before feeling jittery. The aromatic smell would fill the air and everyone would spend the evening in a state of contentment.

Since I always wanted to do whatever the adults were doing, I would ask for a cup of coffee myself. My Mom would put a lot of creamer and sugar in her coffee and I had tasted sips of hers before, so I knew that it was a sweet and creamy beverage and wanted a cup of my own. My Mom would fill my cup with what had to be 95% milk and then add a little bit of coffee and sugar, making up the remaining 5% of my cup, so that I could enjoy it along with the adults. I believe that this was the start of my coffee obsession.

There have never been an abundance of coffee shops in the area where I live. When I was in high school, the neighboring city got a Starbucks and that was huge news for the coffee addicts around me. I would occasionally go there and get a latte or try a new type of coffee blend, but for the most part I still drank a lot of coffee at home. My parents purchased a Keurig coffee maker and have never looked back on the coffee pot they once had. I have tried brewing coffee in many different methods, but to me, a simple pot of coffee still taste the best. It may be that I have too many memories attached to that method of brewing coffee for me to truly ever love any other way.

In college, I had a cheap coffee brewer that would brew a single cup of ground coffee at a time. That machine was pure plastic and a bright red color that didn't really go with anything else, but it worked for what I needed. I also had a French press coffee maker and was prepared to use it often, but upon moving into my dorm room my Mom accidentally knocked it over and it shattered atop the parquet floors. It helped, or didn't depending on how you look at it, that there was a Starbucks on campus.

I had a certain amount of money allotted to me by the college from paying for my dining plan that I could spend at the Starbucks. I quickly discovered that the $150 that was set aside for Starbucks and the other few places to dine on campus would not last me very long. I switched from getting iced chai lattes every day to black coffee with a little cream. It was much more budget-friendly and healthier in the long run.

I had a dining plan which meant that I could eat twice a day in the cafeteria at the school. The food was not bad, but the coffee was atrocious. I believe that I got the coffee once before deciding that I would never get it again. I recall some of my friends getting a cup every time we went to the "dining hall", I would just sit and wonder how they drank it. I suppose if your end goal was to get a buzz off of the caffeine then it wouldn't matter how it tasted, but for me coffee has always been an experience to enjoy.

I would regularly drink my cups of coffee and read books between classes. There has always been something comforting for me in a cup of coffee. Over the years my coffee drinking habits have changed, I don't even drink caffeinated coffee anymore, but still enjoy decaf. However, I believe that for me, a cup of coffee will always serve to represent the possibility of a good conversation and the pausing of time, if only for a moment, where you and your cup of coffee are the only things in the world.

16

GAME BOYS

The Game Boy Color consumed the commercial space on television and it was clear that this would be a big deal. My brother and I wanted one and my parents decided to buy a single handheld gaming system for us. When I say that they bought us "one" that is exactly what I mean. They wanted us to get it and see how well we liked it before getting another.

There was a package deal at Sam's Club where you got the Game Boy Color system and a new game called Pokémon included. Nobody in my family had ever heard of Pokémon before, but the deal was a good one because it was cheaper to buy that package than just the system itself at other retailers. We spent the evening playing the game and immediately it was like we had discovered an entire new world. We had a PlayStation that we had enjoyed for years, but this was our first portable game system.

My parents determined that if they bought another, one for each of us, then it would definitely get used and not be a waste of money. I had a lime green color and my brother had a deep blue for his. I think that the version of Pokémon that I had was Pokémon Red and my brother had Pokémon Blue. That was the start of years and years of entertainment.

Each time that Nintendo would come out with a new portable system, we would want it for a birthday or Christmas gift. We always wanted the new system from Nintendo. Any time that a new Pokémon game was announced we would go to GameStop and pre-order it. There was almost always some type of pre-order bonus, like a small fold-out poster or something, and we actually worried that they may sell out and we wouldn't get a copy if we didn't order in advance.

First thing when I got home from school each day I would grab whatever system was Nintendo's current one and spend hours playing the latest Pokémon game. I had headaches almost every day from staring at the tiny screen for so long, but time flew by when I played that game and I didn't see any good reason that I shouldn't keep playing. There were many times when my parents made me stop playing because they knew it wasn't healthy.

The opening lines of the Pokémon theme song say, "I want to be the very best, like no one ever was." It was that mindset that I, along with millions of others, had when it came to playing the game. You couldn't become the best if you didn't put in the effort of training your Pokémon.

I started noticing that the things I learned in the game were spilling over into my education. Many of the characters had names that were derived from some complex meaning or a root-word that plays into some alternate concept. I would hear a word in science class and immediately be able to derive meaning from the characters in the game. For example, there was a Pokémon called Geodude. When we learned about geodes in class I already had a good understanding of the word. Another quick example is one of the attacks for a water type Pokémon called *hydro pump*. Through that I learned that hydro was another word for water that could also be a prefix for other words relating to water.

My cousin also played the game. He had a special edition Yellow Game Boy Color and the Yellow version of the Pokémon game. That version of the game was unique because the character Pikachu would actually follow your character around on the screen as you adventured through the game. To my knowledge, that was the only Pokémon in that particular version that could follow you around.

We would even take our games on vacation with us. The car ride to wherever we were going was always super short when I was playing the game. We had a vacation coming up where my cousin, aunt, and uncle would be staying in a cabin with us in Pigeon Forge, Tennessee.

I was excited for this because it meant that my brother and I would get to play Pokémon with our cousin, Jeremiah, the entire trip. We gathered the additional cables required to connect one game system to another so that we could battle and trade Pokémon, a ton of extra batteries, and then we were ready to go.

A few days before the trip, my Dad needed to pick up some supplies from a local lumber yard. I waited in the car with my Mom and brother, playing my Pokémon game on my bright lime Game Boy. I caught an Abra, a psychic Pokémon, and remember being elated that I had discovered something so cool. I was looking forward to trading on the trip but I wasn't sure I would want to part with my new Pokémon.

It was a fun trip, and believe it or not, we didn't spend the entire time on our game systems. During the day, we would do touristy things like shop and visit attractions, while in the evenings we somehow still had the energy to play the game. My cousin traded my brother a Pokémon that I wanted, just to make me mad. He had a Ninetales and I desperately wanted it, so he traded it to my brother. Looking back on this, it is funny how much I cared about little things like that.

My cousin and I always had little arguments, though they never latest long because we were very close. Teachers tried to separate us in school because they wanted us to make other friends, so when we argued it was generally over something insignificant and it would always end with us moving on from it shortly after.

I wouldn't call myself a "gamer", but I suppose that back then I fit the description. It was an exciting time for portable game systems because it seemed that the sky was the limit for what would come next. Everyone I knew had some kind of game system, the most popular being the Game Boy Color. I have had game systems that I liked more since then, but if I had to pick a favorite it would be my lime green Game Boy Color because that was the start of so many years of exciting moments playing games and wondering what could possibly happen next.

17

BIRTHDAY DINNERS

One thing that I have always remembered from childhood was that about a week before my birthday each year, my Nanny and Papaw would take me out to dinner to celebrate. They would almost always bring my brother along to celebrate too, and they did the same for his birthdays.

They always let us choose a place that we wanted to eat, and no matter which place we picked they would take us there for a dinner. There was a Chinese restaurant at our local mall called Young Chows that I would usually choose as the place that I wanted to eat. I liked it because it was so different from all of the other places to choose from.

The inside was dimly lit with international décor that made it stand out in my mind as a child. I also loved that the owners of the restaurant would always give me some small gift from their store that was built in to the inside of the place. One year they gave me a small rabbit statue that was covered in fur. It was a little black and white rabbit that stood beside of a mushroom. I can still picture it vividly in my mind.

The thing that made that place so special was that the owners of the restaurant made it a point to talk with each guest who would dine there. It was rare for them not to be standing outside the entrance greeting people as they walked by. They had a passion for their business and that it was important for me to support that, even at a young age.

On days that I was at the mall, not planning to eat there, I would still find my eyes glancing over the international goods that they would sell in the shop portion of the place. One time I bought Yu-Gi-Oh! Cards from their store. Every card was metallic as if it were a special edition and they gave me an excellent price on them. I doubt they ever made much money from the store because they sold things so cheap, just wanting to share their culture and passion with the people of their community. As an adult, I realize that the cards I bought were fakes, but it didn't matter to me at the time, I was not a collector, but merely a kid who was grateful for the kindness of these strangers.

Years later, they would have to shut down over multiple issues. At one time there was a water leak that threatened to ruin the interior of the place. I hoped that they were able to salvage the ornate wall art and room dividers that I once stared at in amazement. Perhaps the thing that led to them closing the restaurant was the news reported many years later that stated they were serving deer meet that they had purchased from a customer instead of meet from an authorized source. I don't know how true any of that was, but it quickly spread and they announced that they were closing shortly after.

It is strange to think of all of the people that play a role in a person's life, even if it is a small one. I didn't know the owners of the restaurant personally, but I can still picture the woman that owned it tidying the souvenirs that they always kept in stock, hoping that someone would buy something, and waving hello to each person that would pass by their beloved business. It makes me wonder how often I am thought of when people recall memories from their past.

We don't actively think of how we are a part of everyone's story that we come in contact with, but there is no doubt in my mind that we are. It is so important to at least be aware of this fact because when we are remembered it will hopefully be for something good. I doubt that I would have remembered that woman in such detail had she stayed in the back of the restaurant managing her staff the majority of the time, or if she had just stood silently at the door only greeting those who would be paying customers. Every little thing that we do matters to someone.

My Nanny and Papaw have always enjoyed buffets, so the fact that that place offered a buffet was also nice. We would spend a long time filling our plates with different types of foods and then talking over our meals as we ate. There was an old ice cream machine that hummed off to the side, greeting you as you made your way to the dessert section. I recall the food being excellent, but I attribute most of that to the company that surrounded me on those simple trips out for a birthday dinner.

18

WHO AM I

Over the years, I have gone through many different phases of what I imagined I would be doing for my career. One day I heard someone talking about marine biology and decided that I wanted to be a marine biologist without actually knowing what one does. I had never even been to the ocean before at that time, yet I had decided that I would someday have a career that directly involved it. That phase lasted a few years.

Next came the phase where I had decided that I would be an actor or something like that, because they seemed to make really good money and it looked pretty fun. I think this was inspired by my love for movies. Don't get me wrong, I was open to the idea of also being famous for anything else entertainment-related. I would just as happily take a recording contract over a movie deal.

It was my fifth-grade year and my school was holding

auditions for the show choir and I wanted to be a part of it. They got to go on a trip each year to perform somewhere really awesome. It was rumored that they would be going to Carowinds Amusement Park in North Carolina to perform and spend the day. I had to audition!

The excitement of possibly going to Carowinds with the group was too much for me. When I went in for my audition, I was to sing in front of my music teacher and her husband. I had never met her husband and felt uncomfortable standing alone in the room with the both of them. My music teacher had a reputation for being mean, though I now realize she wasn't, and I was unsure that I could sing for the two of them.

She was looking for a paper in her files and had turned her head. Her husband, an actual adult, stuck his finger in his nose and started digging around. It was disgusting and I hoped that she was simply unaware of his dirty habit. He pulled his finger out of his nose and licked whatever he had found in there off of his finger. I could not believe that this was one of the two people who would determine if I got to go to Carowinds…I mean, be in the show choir.

She either found the paper that she was looking for or had simply given up on looking for it.

She sighed, "Ok, you can sing any song that you would like to."

I have always been apprehensive about telling people my favorite songs because I feel that music reveals a lot about a person. People make assumptions about all sorts of things, your music preferences included. My nerves were already a mess and now I had to sing a song, one that I was sure they would assume said something about me, and I wasn't sure that I could do it. I don't remember the song that I had in mind, I just know that I was very self-conscious about sharing personal details with strangers and that included singing them a song.

I opened my mouth and nothing came out. I tried again and couldn't do it. I know that they could tell that I wanted in the choir, but they just couldn't let me in without an audition. Her husband seemed as if he could care less if I got in or not, but she seemed distraught.

"It's ok, you can audition next year." She said, ending my audition and chances of going to Carowinds.

I left the room feeling terrible. I was disappointed in myself. My parents were waiting for me and asked how it went.

"Did you get in?" They asked.

There were other people around and I didn't want to embarrass myself any more than I already had.

"I'll tell you in the car." I said.

They were suspicious but agreed to let me tell them about it once we got to the car. I told them about how I had frozen, not actually believing it myself. My parents knew how much I wanted to get in, so my Dad went back in to the school to speak with the music teacher and try to explain. They agreed to let me have another chance at auditioning, and that time I did sing. I was off-pitch and didn't sound great, my nerves still getting the better of me, but it was enough for her to decide to let me in.

It was about this time that my school announced that we would be having a talent show involving all grade levels. I went home and told my parents about it.

"I don't think I want to do it." I said.

"You have to do it." Mom told me.

"Yeah, I think it's a good idea." Dad replied.

I had secretly wanted to do it, but I liked to try and make it seem like it was my parent's idea, this way if something went wrong, I could just say that I never wanted to do it in the first place.

"I guess…" I said reluctantly.

The next order of business was deciding what talent I would compete with. We were supposed to tell the school what we would be doing for the talent show on the day we registered. The obvious choice, that I believe all but a handful of students opted for, was to sing a song. There were quite a few entries into the talent show and a general atmosphere of excitement.

I decided to sing a song by the Christian group Casting Crowns. The song was called "Who Am I". I wasn't sure that it would be a very popular choice among my fellow students, as country music seemed to be the preference, but I went ahead with it anyway.

I practiced that song so many times that I knew every word by heart. I tried singing different parts of the song in various ways, settling on how I would sing it come the day of the talent show. The winner of the show would receive a large trophy saying that they had won. There was no prize money or gifts for winning, just the satisfaction that you had competed against the rest of your school and won. Pretty much everyone wanted the trophy.

The day of the talent show arrived, and I was surprised by how many people had showed up. The students were all there because it was held during school hours, and there were a lot of parents and grandparents that had showed up as well. Both of my parents were there to watch and support me, and since my little brother was only a year behind me in school he was there too. There were people entered into the talent show that I would never have imagined performing for an audience, myself included.

Waiting for my turn was the worst part. I waited backstage, which was little more than a storage hall used for old gym equipment and folded-up metal chairs. The song "Concrete Angel" was sung by at least five students in a row, followed by "Suds In the Bucket", and a duet of "I've Got You Babe". It was clear that my song choice did not fit the theme of the talent show.

It was getting closer and closer to the time that I was supposed to go on. I had heard about people having "butterflies in their stomach" before, but until then I had never fully understood it. I felt like I was going to throw up. Finally, they announced my name and the teacher directing us to go on stage told me that it was my turn. It would not have mattered if it were the largest stage in the world, I could not have felt more nervous than I did at that moment.

I went on stage and when the soundtrack started, I began to sing. I don't remember much about the actual performance, but I have seen the video that my parents recorded and I didn't seem as nervous as I felt. When the song had finished there was applause and I exited the stage. The rest of the performances were more enjoyable because I knew that I had already gone and didn't have anything to worry about at that point except for not winning.

Once everyone had performed, the three judges took time to debate over who they thought should win. Finally, they decided that they had a tie for first place, it was between me and the duet group. I was shocked as I never expected to be considered as the winner. They told us that they needed us to come back that evening to perform in a final round and they would determine the winner then. My parents took my brother and I to Captain D's to celebrate afterwards, even though I had technically tied for first place.

I returned that evening along with the other contestants. Though the other contestants knew they were not being considered for the finals, they came back to perform for their families. I performed once more, much less nervous than before, and after some more debating by the judges, they announced that I was the winner of the whole talent show! I couldn't believe that I had won, it was a very surreal moment for me.

Later, my third-grade teacher told me that she had chills

hearing me sing that song. I never imagined that it would have such an impact. It was an event that I will remember for the rest of my life. Though I have since given up on the idea of having a career in the entertainment industry, I feel content with my shining talent show trophy.

19

LET'S GO TO THE BEACH

The go-to vacation destination for my family has always been Pigeon Forge, Tennessee for as long as I can remember. For years that is what I had come to expect from vacations. It was and is still a place where my family has always been able to get away for a few days, enjoy some stress-free time together, and not have to travel too far.

One year, when I was around nine or ten years old, we decided to go to the beach instead. I had never been to see the ocean before so I was very excited by this idea. I remember we received lots of pamphlets and papers in the mail about different hotels and condos that we could stay at, different places to eat, and general vacation itinerary guides. Booking and planning a vacation online was not popular at all during those days, in fact we did not own a computer at the time.

Like most children, my brother and I had the habit of asking how much longer we had to drive to get to our destination. I mean we even asked this on our trips to Tennessee where we knew pretty much how much longer we would have to wait. We were told by our Dad that the drive to the beach would be much longer than what we normally were used to. We didn't care because we were going to Myrtle Beach, South Carolina to see the ocean.

The first few hours went pretty well. I was small enough at the time that I could comfortably make myself at home in the back seat of the car and go to sleep, however I was also young enough that doing so was no easy task. My mind was reeling with thoughts of how amazing the ocean would look once we got there. Growing up in the mountains, the closest that I ever came to the ocean before then had been seeing a large lake.

We kept driving and driving and driving and... eventually my Dad's frustration was visible. I looked out of the window at the swampy land around me and the residential houses that were falling in on themselves. There was no doubt about it, we were lost and it was possible that we were in a swamp.

"I'm hot..." I said, over and over until my Dad told me to roll the window down. There was very little breeze to comfort me, even with the window rolled all the way down, as we drove through the seemingly endless swamplands. We had to have drove through that area for at least an hour when a large bumblebee flew in my open window and stung me right on the neck.

I started screaming and crying, I'm sure that it sounded like I had just been stabbed. My Dad quickly stopped the car to see what was wrong. The bumblebee must have flown out of the window after it stung me because I do not recall it being anywhere in the back seat after that. I have been stung by quite a few bees in my lifetime, but I recall this one hurting the worst. After some time they had calmed me down and we continued our drive. At this point I am sure that my Dad just wanted to get us out of the swamp.

We finally found the interstate again and were on our way to sunny Myrtle Beach. Only, it was not so sunny when we got there. We drove along the strip until we got to the hotel that we had booked and were relieved that we could get out of the car and finally start our vacation. The skies overhead were angry and gray, threatening a vicious storm, but we didn't care because the ocean was nearby and surely rain was common near the ocean.

Our room was far up in the high-rise hotel that we had booked. From the outside it looked very promising, but the inside was a different story. We got to our room and noticed immediately that some things were not...as advertised. The floors were a white tile material that made any dirt or grime very visible, this did not help things. There was hair on the tile floors, lots and lots of hair. Just about every corner of the room was spotted with a different kind of hair from a previous guest or animal.

In the middle of the wall was a gaping hole.

Had someone gotten mad and punched a hole in the wall?

Why had the hotel just left it there?

There had been absolutely no attempt to clean the room before we arrived or hide the hole in the wall for that matter. Since this was before hotels could receive reviews online, they tended to get away with a lot more and pass off horrendous rooms to unsuspecting vacationers from far away who had booked based on the promise of a professionally taken photo in a travel magazine. It was clear that we would not be staying there.

My Dad argued with the front-desk staff until they refunded us for the room. It was evening now and for whatever reason, almost all of the hotels around were completely booked. I recall Dad saying something about just turning around and going back home, he was understandably frustrated by the entire trip thus far. We saw a vacancy sign lit up at a Super 8 as we drove by and decided to give it a try. After all, it couldn't be any worse than the place we had just come from.

We had gone from a high-rise hotel to a one-floor Super 8 that was designed in a "U" shape with a pool in the middle. The Super 8 was nothing special, but it was clean and that seemed to be all that we could hope for in the moment. We had still not even managed to see the ocean and the weather would ensure that we would have to wait a bit longer to do that. Rain poured ferociously from the sky, pelting the ground with vengeance.

When the rain finally stopped we took the opportunity to finally see the ocean. This was it, the glorious moment that I had been waiting for. We had to pay a pretty steep fee to park near the beach and then we had to walk about five minutes or so to get to the sand. The sky was still gray, and would remain so for pretty much the entirety of our trip, but I would ignore that for the chance to see the clear blue ocean waters that I had dreamed of.

We stood looking at the dark waters crashing to the sand before us. The ocean was as unwelcoming as the sky. We stepped into the rough waters, gravely crushed shells digging into our bare feet, and felt icy shivers run through our bodies as the frigid waves knocked us around. This was not at all like the pictures in the vacation catalogs. Whomever Myrtle Beach had doing their catalogs at the time deserved an enormous pay raise because they had succeeded in bringing us all this way to stand in chilly waters on a gray sunless beach.

The next day the sky was not as gray as the day before, but there was the looming threat of rain pretty much the entire trip. Occasionally, a ray of sun would claw its way past the clouds and give us hope that it isn't always gloomy at Myrtle Beach. My parents tried their best to make it a fun vacation for us. They bought us boogie boards from a small souvenir shop that mostly sold seashells and dried out starfish. We had quite a bit of fun just splashing around in the water with those, and it was a huge plus that our hotel had a swimming pool that we could spend a lot of time in.

Things were looking up and, even though it wasn't the vacation of our dreams, we were determined to make the best of it. We were back at the ocean the next day, and it had rained a lot the night before so we wanted to spend some time at the beach before the next downpour. We were splashing and having fun when my brother walked out of the water and said that something had stung him. He has never been one for being overly dramatic when he Is hurt, so often times it is difficult to tell how bad something is with him.

I am the opposite. When I am hurt, everyone tends to know it. My brother on the other hand is generally calm and reserved.

"I think I saw a jellyfish swim by me." He told my Mom.

"Are you sure?" She said.

There did not appear to be anything wrong with his leg, no swelling or red spots, but we packed up and went back to the hotel just to be safe. Later that evening his leg had big swollen whelps on it and he was visibly in pain. My Dad asked the staff at the front counter of our hotel what can be done for a jellyfish sting, expecting that we would ultimately end up in the emergency room. They told him to buy some meat tenderizer at the grocery store and put it on the area where my brother had been stung.

I remember that we followed their recommendation, and also got some ointments as well, and it cleared up after a few days. We didn't realize it then, but apparently stormy weather can bring jellyfish closer to the shore. After a quick search online, I recently discovered that there is actually science behind why meat tenderizer can help with the pain caused by a jellyfish sting.

We returned home shortly after that. None of us were sad

to be waving goodbye to Myrtle Beach. Though I have had many trips to other beaches since then, never returning to Myrtle Beach, that have been fantastic, I still recall that particular vacation when I think about my first time seeing the ocean. It is not a nightmare to recall like one might expect, rather it is a reminder that no matter where I am, or what tragedies befall me, as long as I am with my family I can make it through the figurative and literal storm safely.

20

I READ THAT IN A BOOK

I never really liked to read in elementary school, that is until my fourth-grade year. That class was possibly one of the most educational and exciting that I have ever taken. My teacher was also an artist and as cliché as it sounds, she made learning fun. There was a chair that was decorated to look like a royal throne. Everyone wanted to sit in that chair, but only the student of the week would get to. She did a great job at keeping it fair so that most all of the students go to sit in that chair at least once during the school year.

Aside form the really amazing chair, you could earn french fries for your McDonalds fry box and depending on whoever had the most at the end of the week you might get to reach into the candy bucket and pull out a handful of candy or get in the mystery prize box. The french fries were clothespins painted yellow, but the McDonalds fry boxes were the real ones from the store that had been donated to the class for this purpose. The girl who sat beside of me in class was always my fiercest competition, but we both wanted to ensure that whoever won that week did so fairly.

There was an instance where we saw a boy taking clothespins from other student's fry boxes and putting them in his own. It didn't take long for both of us to tell the teacher about it. She counted the yellow clothespins one-by-one, determining that he did indeed cheat.

"Thank you for telling me." She said.

We were both proud of the fact that we were helping to keep order in the classroom. Never underestimate how much of a difference in student engagement a simple rewards system can make. I don't know if I was engaged in every lesson because I wanted to win so badly or if I really enjoyed all of the content, but I remember learning a lot in that class.

"Class, we are going to be reading a novel soon." Our teacher said.

I always dreaded the word "novel", it sounded so daunting. All that I had been reading up to that point were the stories in the textbook and they were truly bad enough. I pictured an enormous tome that massed hundreds of pages. My heart sank because I knew that this might be what caused me to lose the prize that week.

I reluctantly joined the rest of the class on the reading rug as we gathered around the teacher's rocking-chair. The book she was holding was nowhere near as big as I had thought it would be, in fact it looked quite manageable.

"The book is called Because of Winn-Dixie." She said.

She could have easily played the audiobook version of the story for us to listen to, but instead she read it aloud each day during reading time until we were finished. I was disappointed as the reading for the day would end and I would have to wait until the next day to find out what happened next. That was the first time that I recall being so engaged in a story. I believe that is the moment when the seed for my love of reading was planted.

The next time that I was engrossed in a book would be two years after the reading of "Because of Winn-Dixie". As part of our sixth grade English class we would get to choose an R.L. Stine Goosebumps book to read and write a report on. I loved this assignment because I had always enjoyed the Goosebumps series of books. I had never read one all of the way through up to that point, but I had seen all of the television episodes and just knew if they were anything like the show, I would enjoy them.

When it was my time to choose which Goosebumps book I would be reading, I picked one called "Stay Out of the Basement". The cover was purple and had a monster on the front with tree limbs and roots growing from it. There was also the element of an experiment happening because the monster held a beaker and was surrounded by a scientific atmosphere. I was happy with my choice as I found that I enjoyed the book immensely.

It would be a few more years before I would read another book by choice. One of my friends always carried around books with them. It was about the time that the Twilight craze was happening, and she had brought that book to school with her. I recall the book standing out because of its stark black cover with the hands holding an apple.

"What book is that?" I asked.

"*Twilight*. It's about vampires and stuff but it is also a romance." She said.

I was interested when she said vampires, but knew that I probably wouldn't finish it if it was too much of a romance. I got the book but never finished it, I was right in assuming that it wouldn't be the type of book that I would enjoy. I decided to get another book to bring with me to school and read, this time one that I picked on my own without any recommendation from anyone else.

I had just seen the movie Eragon and really liked it. Despite the fact that there were never any sequels to the movie, I knew that there was a book series and thought that if the movie was good, the book would surely be better. I got the edition of the book that had the movie poster design as its cover. I do not like when they put the movie posters as the book cover design, but I must admit to owning a few over the years. I never finished that book either, but I did carry it around with me for months.

About that time, I started working in my school's main office. I did things like make copies, answer the telephone, and sign people in when they entered the building. There was a lot of down time with this job as my school was pretty small. I had gotten an Amazon Kindle for Christmas, one of the ones that read like paper, and purchased "The Hunger Games". I devoured that book and the others in the series while working in my school's office.

There have been along of periods in my life, each seemingly accentuated by a book or group of books that I read. Looking back, so many of my memories are tied to what I was reading at the time. For example, I clearly recall reading "How To Lead A Life of Crime" and "Tokyo Heist" the summer that I worked for a non-profit educational program at the university I was attending.

I remember a frigid day when I was walking to my Nanny and Papaw's house with my parents, "The Tale of Desperaux" tucked away in my coat so that it wouldn't get ruined by the snow, and my Dad hugging me and unknowingly making me drop the book which made me angry. I feel bad for being so mad about dropping that book and denting the spine a little because it doesn't really matter what is on the outside of a book, but what matters are the words contained upon the pages, still and unmoving until the reader gives them a moment of attention.

You might wonder what I was doing during my senior year of college, but you would be better off asking me what books I was reading. Thinking back to the stories that have filled my life over the years, these are the ones that I have allowed to become a part of me. So few things stand the test of time, but ink on paper has seemed to weather the years better than most. I write my memories because as the ink on paper fades, so do the stories of our lives. One day these moments may only be text on a page. One day, when recalling my life, I may say, "I read that in a book." The words will be as true as I have always known them to be.

21

CORNSTALK NINJA

Growing up, computers were not the influence that parents worried about. We didn't have cellphones to occupy our time, but we did have one thing that tended to be our source of cultural influence. I watched quite a lot of television as a child. I was always fascinated by the cartoons on Nickelodeon, I didn't even know there was a Disney Channel until I was in middle school. My favorite shows were Cat Dog, The Angry Beavers, Hey Arnold!, Rugrats, and just about anything else that came on Nickelodeon.

One day, my uncle had some cornstalks that he had thrown across the road from his house. I don't recall what he had been using them for, perhaps some type of fall or Halloween decoration. The air outside was crisp and cool, the promise of a cold winter looming in the near distance. My cousin lived next door, so when my brother and I went outside to play as children, he was almost always there too. The three of us did a lot of things together growing up, and I am grateful for the fact that we were able to live right beside of one another.

We had decided to take the cornstalks and use them as ninja swords. I don't know if "ninja swords" is the correct technical term, but for children, that term did suffice. It didn't take us very long to realize that cornstalks could also be very dangerous. I always hear stories of how people's children get into crazy predicaments and get injured doing seemingly nonsensical things, but as a child who was taught how to avoid trouble, I still found myself battling my brother and cousin with a cornstalk one autumn day.

Our battle quickly turned from being causal to one of intensity. I brought the cornstalk down on my brother's foot and recall him letting out a loud cry of pain. When we looked down, we could see that his toe had been split open from the edge of the cornstalk. We quickly threw our ninja swords down on the ground and rushed him inside where we were scolded for playing with them in the first place.

If you are worried about my brother, don't be; his toe healed and he has no scars to show for the incident. The reason that this story stands out for me is because it was a seemingly harmless decision that turned dangerous. I try to be understanding when I hear about kids who do things that sound ridiculous to adults, because telling this story as an adult makes me realize that I have learned a few things over the years.

22

AWKWARD

I was unsure how to title this chapter because the story that I am about to tell is a strange one. I just want you to know that I am not exaggerating or making any of this up. What you are about to read actually happened.

It has been said that you will never forget your first kiss. From my experience, that is true, especially when it comes as a shock. My family and I had been attending a church that was fairly close to where we lived at the time. For the first few weeks, everything was pretty normal.

I remember going to the basement where they had Sunday School for the children and the pastor's wife teaching us lessons. The walls were painted white and the windows that were close to the ceiling let in quite a bit of light, so for a basement it didn't feel much like one.

There weren't many kids in our Sunday School class as it was a small church with a small congregation. When Vacation Bible School would come around it would be a completely different story, children from everywhere would attend and I often wondered why I would only see them once a year over the summer. The pastor's daughter was in the class with my brother and I, and it was clear that she liked me.

I was still pretty young at the time, I would say around ten years old, and I was not interested in dating anyone. You had me, a kid who was happy with things the way they were, and you had her, a girl who was determined to have a boyfriend because that's what Disney Channel had told her she needed. The way she acted was almost like a character from one of the Disney shows, very over-the-top and precisely the way that the television portrayed boy-crazy girls.

After a few Sundays, she asked me to be her boyfriend. I told her that I didn't want to. Normally, that would be the end of that conversation, and often times the relationship of acquaintance would follow. However, she was one of the most determined people that I had ever met and was not willing to give up so easily. It had also become clear that her parents were aware of her goals to make me her boyfriend because they would always have very bright smiles when they spoke to act this way towards the other children.

You might wonder why I refer to myself as a child at age ten, it is because I pretty much see anyone under the age of thirteen as a kid and anyone above thirteen years of age as a teenager. She continued to ask me to date her just about every chance that she got, and I continued to tell her that I wasn't interested. It became very annoying and I got to the point that I tried to avoid being around her at all costs.

One day, we were attending church for an evening service. My parents always seemed to end up in conversations with her parents after the service. Sometimes it felt like we were there an extra hour or two after the service ended while they had conversations. My brother and I would usually talk to one another or play a game or something to occupy ourselves. This particular evening was different from the others.

It was a summer evening so there was still a faint glow to the darkening sky. I was walking around the exterior of the church, examining the rocks or whatever I could find to keep my mind busy. The pastor's daughter was outside too, she tended to be wherever I was. I would walk to a spot along the side of the church and she would suddenly decide that she wanted to walk there too.

I had always been very nice and polite to her, and perhaps that was the problem. I am not the type of person to default to being rude with someone because they are bothering me.

"I'm just going to walk on ahead, you can stay here." I said.

"No, it's fine I can walk too." She wouldn't take the hint.

We were coming to the corner of the church when I felt her push me up against the brick wall. I was completely caught off guard and confused. The next thing I knew, she was pressing her lips onto mine and having a very one-sided kiss. As soon as she had started, she had ended. She took off running and disappeared.

I tried to unravel the events that led to this moment and then I tried to comprehend what this meant. I wasn't her boyfriend, in fact I thought that I had made it abundantly clear to her that I didn't want to ever be her boyfriend, yet she quite literally stole my first kiss from me. This was a time before I knew much about anything, yet in some ways I knew more than I do now. To me, this was a very big deal and I was angry with her for taking it so lightly.

I told my parents that night when we got home, and they were not happy about it either. They told her parents, which made things even worse because she was even more persistent after that. Years would go by before she would wear me down and I would agree to date her. I honestly got to the point where I was exhausted with the whole thing and thought that it couldn't make things any worse if I just gave her what she wanted and dated her.

I was very wrong and that one mistake of agreeing to date her led to many more years of stress. There were some days that I would convince myself that she was just behaving normally and that I really shouldn't be considering a restraining order, but then there were others where I would have to spend the evening texting her to explain why we would NEVER work. I didn't like feeling forced into the "relationship" and to this day, I see the whole thing as extremely awkward.

When I finally broke up with her, I started getting threatening text messages from her best friend. I knew that she was behind the messages, trying to force me to go back to dating her, but I did not give in that time. The messages threatened to kill me, specifically with knives, and I have to admit that her best friend was a frightening person. I only felt relief knowing that I was finally able to end the relationship and eventually cut ties with her altogether.

I was never serious about dating her, so I always knew that it would never amount to anything, but there were times that the stress of feeling trapped got to me. I understand how some people find it difficult to leave bad relationships, especially when the other person simply won't take "No" for an answer. So, after much consideration, I think that I will title this chapter, "Awkward" because it really does sum up that whole story.

My advice to you is to never get into a bad relationship, if you feel that it isn't right then you need to trust your instincts. If you happen to be the person having a hard time accepting a rejection, just consider how uncomfortable it might make the other person to have to continually say "No". We possibly could have been good friends had things never happened the way that they did, so just consider the relationship you might be ruining by not taking the other person's decision into account. Just don't make things...awkward.

23

A VISION OF PASSING

I have never been a huge fan of the dark. I would not say that I am afraid of the dark, rather what might be lurking in it. A lot it this probably stems back to my overactive imagination as a child. I have always found it difficult to stop my mind from running wild with thoughts.

I don't have nearly as many nightmares as I did when I was younger. I wouldn't say that they were a regular occurrence, but they definitely happened about once a week. Sometimes, in the blurry state between being awake and being asleep, I would find it hard to tell what was real and what was simply part of my dream-state. One dream that I remember vividly from when I was a child took place in a setting of nothingness.

There was a void and then suddenly dry-gray ground beneath where I stood. I did not notice the giant Roman columns all around until my attention was drawn to one by a large owl with a menacing look on its face. Imagine the Parthenon without a roof or floor, only the columns remaining and at unevenly spaced intervals. The owl stared at me with knowing eyes, unwilling to let me in on whatever secret it was holding on to.

Next, I was being chased by something that I could not remember upon waking. I ran through the columns even though I knew that it was pointless. This place led to nowhere, was nowhere, and would keep me if I ever stopped running. I ran and screamed until I woke, muted cries for help escaping my lips. There have been a few other times over the years that I have awakened myself by screaming so loud in my dreams that I made noises in the real world.

Nightmares are a curious thing. You can know that you are in one, but that doesn't make them any less frightening. One's own mind knows what horrors can terrify you the most effectively, and on the nights it sees fit, it can torment you with vengeance. Only, what I am about to tell you was no nightmare, it was something that I was awake to experience.

Being no more than ten years old, the summer months were always some of my favorites. There was a fan in the hallway pointed towards my bedroom, the fan helped me sleep during the summer when the temperatures tended to be hot. I have always liked having a fan going at night, even if I have to burrow under three layers of blankets to get comfortable. I closed my eyes, the fan circulating warm-cool air, and I drifted off to sleep. Time has a funny way of working when you are sleeping. It felt like I had just fallen asleep when I had the sense that someone was watching me.

My eyes shot open and I dared not move, as if laying absolutely still would ever help in a situation where I was actually in harm's way. I laid like that for a few minutes and then slowly pushed myself up with my arms. I looked out into the hallway, expecting to see just the fan spinning quietly, but that is not what I saw. There was something white walking on all fours. When it sensed that I was looking back at it, it stood up, a slight hunch in it's posture, and stared directly at me.

Bright red eyes stood out in contrast to it's stark white body. My heart rate soared and I could feel my pulse racing. I thought to myself that I had to be asleep, that this had to be a nightmare. I closed my eyes tightly for a moment and then opened them. The thing was still standing in the hallway, eyes fixed on mine. I stared at it, not wanting to let it out of my sight, for if I did I could not imagine what it might be capable of.

I did not have a good feeling about this thing, I got the sense that it was sinister and not here for anything good. I watched it until I couldn't stay awake any longer and then fell asleep. It would be years before it would return to watch me again.

The next time that I saw it, it stood in the hallway in the middle of the night once again. It was summer of 2007 and I was thirteen years old. It had been years since the first occurrence but I knew immediately that it was the same thing returning. I had a sense of dread in my stomach that this time it was back for a reason. Those red eyes gleamed in the darkness, the white and red becoming the center of my focus.

I spent another long night waiting to fall back into sleep. I was exhausted from staying awake that night and had planned to sleep in until the sun woke me up, but my Mom woke me with some terrible news. My uncle had died. My uncle lived beside of our house and at the time he was living by himself. After the ambulance came and took his body away, we were later told that he had died of a drug overdose. They said that he had the phone nearby and had attempted to call 9-1-1, but he was unable to finish dialing the number.

My aunt and uncle had always been there, and to find out that one of them was gone was devastating. Any time that you lose someone, especially a family member, it is difficult. I still wonder if the thing that I saw in the hallway was there to warn me of what was to come, or if I had been able to interpret the meaning of why it was there if things could have been different. It may be that seeing it the night that my uncle passed away was a coincidence, but I have always believed that there are deeper meanings to things. Maybe the thing was not malevolent after all, maybe it was trying to warn me, I doubt that I will ever know. I just hope that I never see it again, even in a dream.

24

ROCKET POWER

I spent many evenings watching cartoons as a child. I would rush home from school, grab an armful of junk food, and turn on the television. The only channel worth watching was Nickelodeon because that was where all of the good cartoons were. I watched hundreds of episodes of CatDog, The Angry Beavers, Rugrats, and of course, Rocket Power.

One of my favorite shows was Rocket Power. It was great, just a bunch of kids who were awesome at skating, biking, rollerblading, and pretty much any other outdoor sport you could think of. Luckily, this show encouraged me to spend some time outdoors too. No, I didn't spend my entire childhood sitting in front of a television, in fact quite a lot of it was spent outdoors.

My brother and I, along with the other kids that lived nearby, would ride our bicycles and skateboards for hours.

The road that we would ride on was not the safest because it was only big enough for one car at a time and trees and bushes blocked much of our view. We would have someone watch for cars while the others rode and then we would switch off and take turns keeping check, so that we were at least being a little safe.

When I say that we rode skateboards, that is an overstatement. Since none of us knew how to actually ride a skateboard, and there was really no way to ride one on a downward sloping street, we would sit on them and let gravity do the rest. It wouldn't take long to pick up speed because the road was sloped downward. The only problem that we ever had was stopping.

We would use our feet as brakes and if the skateboard would get too fast we would apply more force to the pavement with our feet. The friction would eventually burn through the rubber on the soles of our shoes. I ruined so many pairs of shoes by doing this, but it was a ton of fun so I didn't mind.

One summer evening, I was riding my bicycle. It was a yellow bike with black accents and I rode it in much the same way that I rode the skateboard, the only difference was that I wore a helmet when riding the bike. I would take my feet off of the brakes and let the downward slope propel me forward. I had done this hundreds of times before, so I didn't expect this time to be any different.

The bike was picking up speed, so I tried to engage the brakes. The only problem was that the bike was gaining speed and the brakes did not seem to be working. Panic rushed through me as I wondered how I would possibly come to a stop. If I rode the bike to the end of the road there was a chance that a car would be pulling in and I didn't even take into account the fact that our road led onto the main street where I would be in an even worse situation if I made it that far without being able to stop.

Yes, eventually the bicycle would have to come to a stop if I wasn't peddling it, but how far would I have to go before that happened? In a few moments, I would be near the area before my house and I could get onto the grass and possibly stop if the grass were to cause the bike to slow down. This would have been a great plan for stopping, had I been able to control the bike. I turned onto the grass and tried to move it towards a hill, but I had lost all control of the bike and it was threatening to topple me over. I held onto the handlebars and hoped for the best.

I crashed into a gazebo that was nearby and immediately felt a surge of pain. The bike had stopped, but in the process, it had twisted and caused me to ram one of the handlebars into my groin area. I let out a cry for help and my parents came running. It took a lot of effort to stand after that. When I looked to assess the damage, I saw a purple and yellow whelp forming, about the size of a baseball. My Dad rushed me to the emergency room where we spent the entire evening. It truly did not look good.

Luckily, I survived and did not have any lasting damage from the accident. It took weeks before I was able to walk without being in any kind of pain. I wondered if I would ever feel comfortable riding a bike again?

I stopped riding my bike unless it was on a flat surface. Those kids on Rocket Power made everything look so easy, but that show had an extreme lack of accuracy. One thing they did get right is how much fun it could be to ride a bike or skateboard. I don't know if the brakes were to blame, or my own lack of caution, but one thing is for sure, I don't ever plan to ride a bicycle down a sloped hill ever again.

25
SPIDER CHECK

One night when I was younger, I went to bed like normal, but I didn't realize what was about to happen. I closed my eyes and was ready for sleep. I felt something light brush against my cheek. I didn't think anything of it, but it happened again and then it brushed against my forehead and across the other side of my face.

I jolted awake and ran to the light switch. When I turned on the light there was a massive spider resting on the side of my bed! Chills went through my body, as I have never liked spiders, and I had my Dad come and kill it. I wish that I could say that was the last time that I shared a bed with a spider, but unfortunately it was not.

A few years later, I was half-asleep in bed when I felt something brush against my leg. Again, I didn't think anything of it, but when it kept happening, I turned on the light and pulled back my bedsheets to find a spider. That was the night that I started doing spider checks.

A spider check is basically when you turn down your bed before getting into it, making sure that there are no unwanted guests planning to take a nap with you. I also check my pillows to make sure that nothing has crawled up in the pillowcases.

I read somewhere that the average person swallows a certain number of spiders each year while they sleep. I have done the research and found that this is a myth. For years I believed it, and it has never been one-hundred percent determined to be false, so I still do spider checks. There have been a few nights that I have decided to skip it, and wouldn't you know it, those have been the nights that I have found spiders in my bed.

It is worth mentioning that as I sat down to write this a two-inch black spider crawled past my chair. It startled me because it was extremely fast. I don't know if writing this chapter attracted the spider or not, but just in case I want to be finished with this chapter.

26

BABY SHARK

I believe that I spent many years in my youth preparing to be on the show Shark Tank before it even existed. The reason that I say this is because I have always seemed to have some type of money-making idea that I want to bring to the world. Living in rural West Virginia, I grew up seeing a lack of money in my community. I am fortunate to never have wanted for anything, but I have known people who do. Perhaps it is that understanding of money and its importance in today's society that instilled a passion for business in me at such a young age.

When I would play outside in the summer with my relatives and the other children in the neighborhood, I would construct some type of monetary system for our games. Some days it would be acorns that we would find all over the grassy ground, but there was almost always a currency of some form involved. I always wanted to be the boss or manager in whatever imaginary world we lived in during those days. My "employees", the other children, would collect the acorns and bring them to me so that I could then keep the majority of them and give them a few in return for their troubles.

I don't think there was ever any point to these games other than me learning how business works at a very young age. As everyone grew older, those games did not hold the same appeal as they once did. Instead of working with acorns, and let's be honest they don't hold their value very well on a global scale anyway, I switched to real money.

I believe I was around eight or nine years old at the time when I had started riding the school bus instead of my Aunt and Mom taking me each day. My brother and I adjusted well to riding the school bus and it was only about fifteen minutes from the time school ended until we were off the bus at our stop. One day my uncle gave my brother and I a bunch of school supplies. There were these really cool triangular and rectangular metallic erasers, pencils with all sorts of neat designs, and other supplies that would have looked amazing to a child my age.

I took as much of the school supplies that I could and stuffed it into my lunch bag, my brother doing the same, and we started selling it on the back of the school bus. The idea came to me when one of the kids on my bus commented that they would give me a dollar for one of the metallic erasers. I now realize that a product does not have to be very good, it just has to be shiny for kids to want it. The erasers were probably made out of the cheapest materials possible, but I had a lot of them and saw an opportunity.

My brother and I sold school supplies on the back of the school bus for weeks until our enormous supply had been depleted. There always seemed to be a kid that had a quarter they were willing to part with in exchange for a smiley face pencil.

Trading was also a very popular pastime at my elementary school, and while I was always up for the occasional trade, I much preferred selling things for money. That is the first instance of selling something for money that I can recall.

At home I was always making things to try and sell to my family.

"Look Nanny, I made a set of bookmarks and colored them myself." I would say to my Grandmother.

"Wow, you did?" She would reply.

"Yeah and they are for sale too!"

Over the years, my family bought so much junk from me to support my attempts at entrepreneurship. Things changed when I got to high school and realized that my classmates had jobs and decent amounts of cash that they were always looking to spend.

I opened my first bank account when I was fifteen, my parents co-signing so that I could have the account. I would put small amounts of money into the account and with the accompanying debit card, I would spend it. Cell phones were having a revolution at that time and I remember just about everyone had a Motorola Razr, until they all started getting BlackBerries, and then iPhones.

If you wanted a cool cellphone case, you had to go to one of the many kiosks at the mall that sold them and spend anywhere from $15 to $30 on one. I discovered that you could order cellphone cases easily from eBay at much cheaper prices. If you were willing to wait, then you could get one shipped from China for around $1 or you could pay a little more and get one shipped from the USA (still a case from China but shipped within the USA) for around $4.

I thought that if people were willing to pay $20 for a phone case without hesitating at the mall, then why wouldn't they rather have it delivered directly to them for the same price? It turns out that the students at my school were very willing to pay the same premiums that they were paying at the mall in exchange for buying a phone case from me.

It was not as common for a high school student to have a debit card at the time, so I had the ability to order from a seemingly limitless selection of phone case designs, whereas my classmates who did not have debit cards could only buy from the limited selection of designs at the mall. I sold cellphone cases for a very long time until everyone started getting debit cards and discovering that they could place an order themselves.

When selling phone cases slowed down, I got a group of my friends together and started a small commission-based business, unofficially called Apple Tree Accessories. I would put together catalogs of products that I had sourced from wholesalers in China and the students in my class would pick what they wanted from the catalog. I would then go home and order whatever it was that they wanted and collect the difference between the price I paid and the markup price that I charged.

My friends that sold the products for me from catalogs that I had printed and given to each of them would receive a small percentage of anything they sold. This lasted for a few months until I found reselling from wholesale companies to be too difficult of a task to conquer while also having a part-time job myself outside of school hours. Trust me, if I could have just sold cell phone cases forever at the prices I was charging, that is what I would have done instead.

During this time I had also started making videos on my YouTube channel. The videos were random in content and not very interesting, but it was a hobby that I intended to one day make money from. I figured that if I never made money from it that would be okay because I was having fun while doing it. I also started selling products on Etsy, though I had better luck trading graphic design services where I would design shop banners for sellers on the website in exchange for one of their products for free.

A lot of my attempts at making money from this point in time were technology-based. There was a website that had just been announced called Take180. The idea was that you would submit an entry for a specific challenge, such as inventing a fictional illness, and if your idea won, it would be part of an upcoming video. You would also receive some type of prize in the mail, usually accompanied by a check worth a few hundred dollars. The crazy thing was that when this company started there were very few people using it, I blame their marketing department because it truly was a great idea. I recall winning a handful of their contests and having old family photos as well as some of my ideas featured in their videos. At one point, I believe the website partnered with Shane Dawson, one of YouTube's first stars, to help promote it, but by then they had given away so much money and so many prizes that I assume they went bankrupt.

My YouTube revenue started to pick up to a point where it was providing a nice source of passive income and my other online projects were netting a pretty good amount too. I don't know that I will ever make enough money online to quit working a regular job, or that I would even feel comfortable quitting a job to live off of online income, but I have always thought that it is important to have multiple sources of revenue because you never know when you might need it.

In college, I started a company that sold Japanese candy. At the time, there was a local Sci-Fi convention that I sold at once a year and would make a good amount of money. In between selling at the convention, I would sell often at a local independent bookstore where I had regular customers who would get up early on the weekends just to buy a bag filled with Pocky and Umaibo from me.

Sometimes I would dress like a Pokémon trainer, and one

time my then-girlfriend dressed as Pikachu and helped me sell at one of the events. It was fun because it was not serious and it visibly brought joy to my small corner of the world. I called the business Manga Snack and I hope that someday I can bring it back.

One night during my college years, I was at an open mic night and had another idea for a business. Our college had a paper on campus, but they only reported about what the professors asked them to report on. I like to read and even I had trouble finding the content of the paper interesting. A few of my friends were with me at the open mic and I told them we should start an online magazine and report on what we wanted to. There would be no specific category of content which goes against the rules of creating a successful website, but it would be a fun project that could lead to potential income.

They loved the idea, but none of them wanted to do the work to get it started. I said that I would create the website because I had created many other websites in the past and all that they would need to do would be write content. They agreed and I settled on the name Toast Pop. It was nonsensical, but unique enough that it could actually be a brand. To this day the website still exists, though all of those friends that originally wrote for it have left.

Working online over the years, alongside working multiple in-person jobs, and going to school was not easy. I have always worked hard to ensure that I have a steady stream of stable income and I hope that everyone can learn from these attempts at entrepreneurship that I have made over the years. Success does not come easy to most, it sure hasn't for me, but if you don't try then you will never know the feeling of having one of your ideas come to life and change the world, if only in some small way.

27

CANDY BAR BOOKSTORE

The local mall has had a few different brands of bookstores over the years. I remember when I was very young that there was a Waldenbooks and a Christian Bookstore in the mall. We would almost always go to both when we would visit the mall as at that time we tended to go in just about every store, making a trip to the mall feel like a whole-day event.

The Christian Bookstore was a favorite of my Nanny's because they carried a lot of different kinds of Bibles and gospel soundtracks that she loved to listen to. I think I only ever bought one actual book from there and it was a choose-your-own-adventure book where you would decide what the characters would do next and then turn to whichever page it told you to turn to, so that the story could progress. At the time I thought that was a really amazing concept and even today I still think its not a bad idea for children's books.

By the time that I was in middle school, the Waldenbooks had been turned into a Borders. We would have the Borders bookstore for years until it too closed and finally a Books-A-Million would take its place on the other end of the mall. While in middle school I would spend a lot of time over the weekends at the mall with my friends. My friend group was small, but I didn't mind because we had a lot in common and a good evening could be spent just walking around the mall to have something to do.

One evening I was with my brother and cousin at Borders while my parents were shopping in some other store. The mall wasn't huge, so there was never much worry about getting lost or anything. I was in a phase of reading where all I wanted to read was Manga. I had gotten into the Kingdom Hearts manga and was browsing that section of the store when my French teacher walked by and said hello. My brother was trying to find something that would interest him as he was not (and currently is not) a big reader, but he did like the Goosebumps books, so that was where he stood browsing the shelves.

My French teacher was from Senegal, Africa and had studied in Paris before coming to teach French at my school. I always wondered why he would want to teach at my small school when he had seen so much of the world. I loved having a foreign language teacher who had actually been a foreigner. His class was all the more interesting to me because he had personal experiences that helped make the language come to life.

His family was still in Africa and he was working to be able to bring them here to America to be with him. I felt bad after learning that because even though he was one of the most intelligent people that I had ever met, he was struggling just to bring his family to the place he saw as having the most opportunity. I always assumed that teachers didn't make much money, a suspicion that I have since confirmed, but had I known how little they make I would have felt even worse for him. He never seemed sad though, always happy and eager to share his passion for languages with the class.

The other teachers would normally dress in casual clothes, at most I would call it dress-casual, but he was always dressed as if he was going to be meeting with a group of the most important people in the world. It always made me feel good to walk into a classroom where the teacher took their job of educating us seriously. I wish that I could say that he was respected for his efforts, but he had a very hard time teaching at my school. The students took advantage of the fact that he had an accent and would feign ignorance after he would pour his heart into the lessons. Parents would complain that their students were receiving bad grades in his class because they couldn't understand him.

In reality, he did have an accent, but I never had any trouble understanding him. The complaints were completely unfounded, and he did not deserve to be treated that way. I assume that he still faces similar issues as he continues to teach at the same school that I went to. I wish that he were teaching in a collegiate setting where he could be showed the respect that he is due because, unless the administration demands respect for him, I do not see much changing. It was an easy opportunity for most of the students to get away with doing nothing, while they had the perfect opportunity to learn from someone that they could only ever hope to be as wise as.

We spoke for a moment about books and then my French teacher walked away to browse the store. About ten minutes later, I was still looking at the Manga and my cousin was looking for something good to read in the Young Adult section of the store. My French teacher was at the front counter by then and I assumed that he was paying for a book that he had found. I always imagined that teachers spent their free time reading and doing studious things. Since becoming a teacher, I know that is pretty much true for myself but that this actually applies to a very small percentage of educators.

A moment later, I saw him standing nearby and holding out three candy bars. He had purchased one each for myself, my brother, and my cousin. That moment surprised me because I had never had a teacher give me anything outside of school. I had assumed that he would be saving all of his money so that he could bring his family to America. Perhaps it was knowing that this small purchase would set his goals back ever so slightly that made me appreciate it all the more. He told us to have a good day and then left the store. It was expensive chocolate that I never would have purchased for myself, but he must have noticed that my cousin and I put forth effort in his class and showed him respect as everyone else should have.

He was simply a kind person, and knowing him, I know that there was no motive behind it except for doing a good deed. It caught me off-guard because we are taught from a very early age that the way to get ahead in life is to look out for one's self. We need more small acts of kindness in the world where people do nice things "just because".

I don't know if he realized how much that small act of kindness meant to me, or how I would remember it years later, but it is proof that a little act of kindness can go a long way. I have since learned that his family is now in America with him and his perseverance paid off. I wish that I could say he makes a very good income now from teaching, but the pay for educators is still extremely low. He was, and is, one of the most intelligent people that I have ever met. He is proof that if you are truly intelligent then your knowledge will manifest in small ways that might just be remembered for years and years to come.

28

KENTUCKY FRIED FIRST JOB

I wanted to start working as soon as I possibly could. I always had this idea that the sooner I started working at a job, the sooner I would have loads of money to spend. Since then, I have discovered that a job generally comes with taxes and other expenses that ensure you never make too much money.

My first job was a strange one. I had interviewed for a position at KFC (Kentucky Fried Chicken), and they told me that they normally didn't hire people as young as me. I believe that I was fifteen years old at the time, which meant that I had to get a special work permit from my high school stating that I was responsible enough to have a job. They hired me anyway and I was excited to have my first ever real job!

"I just have to be able to get off work at around 10:00 PM

because I have to get up pretty early for school." I made sure to tell the person interviewing me.

"Ok, that won't be a problem, I'll just schedule your shift to end at either 9:00 PM or 10:00 PM. Occasionally, you may have to work a little later than that, but it won't be often." They replied.

I didn't mention it, but my parents had to drive me to work since I was not old enough to have a drivers license. I had to make sure that they weren't stuck in the parking lot until the late hours of the night waiting on me to finish my shift.

My first day of work there was off to a terrible start when they told me that they needed me to work in the kitchen. I don't want to brag, but I have always been amazing on a cash register and can take people's orders in a fraction of the time it takes most people, so I had hoped to have a job working up front. Nevertheless, I followed them back into the steamy kitchen.

The kitchen was extremely unimpressive and sparse. It seemed to have just the supplies needed to cook the items on the menu and nothing else. The person training me took me directly over to a wide industrial sink and told me that they needed me to wash some dishes. Judging by the way that they said it, I figured I would wash dishes for a few minutes and then be trained on something else once they were clean. What I did not anticipate was that they had not washed dishes in some time, apparently waiting on the new hire to come in for their first shift.

The water was scalding, and I couldn't seem to get the temperature to change. I plunged my hands into the steaming water and began cleaning the greasy pans, washing away leftover bits of raw chicken. As soon as the pile of dishes would start to lessen, someone would come over to the sink and drop off another stack. I quickly realized that the pile of dishes at KFC is never-ending because they cook chicken all day long and need the dishes to be washed as quickly as possible. How they had managed before I arrived was beyond me.

The guy cooking the chicken walked from one side of the kitchen to the other, grabbing the coating of spices for the raw meat. He handled the uncooked chicken without gloves, and I wondered at how sanitary that could be. Surely people at other restaurants wore gloves when they cooked the food.

My hands had turned a bright red color from the scalding water that I had been working with for the past few hours and the dishes seemed to be coming in an endless cycle. I had to lean over to scrub the pans and my back was hurting so bad that I wasn't sure I could even make it to the end of the shift. All of the nerves in my back were screaming for me to stop, call it quits, and walk out the front door. They probably would not have even noticed that I was gone until they needed a fresh pan to throw some chicken carcasses on.

As a supporter of animal rights and a vegetarian, I am amazed that I ever worked there to begin with, but money is money and I wanted to get a paycheck. 10:00 PM rolled around and nobody came to tell me that my shift was over. I had been watching the clock, so I knew that my parents would be outside in the parking lot waiting to pick me up.

"I need to clock out and leave." I told another employee.

She looked at me like it was the first time that they noticed there was a new employee in the room.

"And?" She said.

"Well, I don't know how to clock out."

She laughed and then looked at me pityingly, "Honey, you can't leave until everyone does. We've already locked the doors and we don't unlock them until this place is completely closed down and everyone is ready to go."

"Nobody ever told me that. I was told that I could leave at 10:00 PM and there wouldn't be any problem. I have school in the morning."

She was not fazed by the fact that I would have to go home, shower so that I didn't smell like chicken grease, do homework, and then get an hour or two of sleep before school.

"I mean, you can help us close if you want. The quicker we get done, the quicker you get to leave."

I was angry and felt betrayed. I wouldn't have been so shocked if I hadn't asked the person who hired me if I could leave by 10:00 PM. I did help them close the store and about two hours later I was able to leave. My parents were furious, though there was nothing I could do about what had happened.

I called the next day to tell them that I quit. I didn't even feel bad about it. If they only wanted me to wash dishes they could probably just buy a dishwashing machine and save some time and money in the long run. When I went to pick up my paycheck weeks later, they were rude about giving it to me. Because I hadn't bought into their strange practice of locking employees in the store and forcing them to work longer hours than they were scheduled for, they saw me as a traitor.

I believe that I made around $30 after taxes for my entire evening of work. It would not be the last time that I was in awe of the small number beside of the dollar sign on my paycheck. I don't regret that experience because I feel that we can learn from just about anything. I just hope that since then they have bought a dishwasher and maybe a pair of gloves for whoever is cooking.

29

PART-TIME

Since I started working, I have had many different part-time jobs. A few that I enjoyed, but many that I am thankful to never have to go back to. I think that going in chronological order would be best, so I will begin by skipping over KFC (Kentucky Fried Chicken), since you already know about that one, and move on to the next.

After leaving KFC, I got a call for an interview at none other than Chick-Fil-A. I wasn't sure why every job opportunity I was receiving involved chicken, but even though I didn't want to be type-casted as someone who only works at places selling chicken, I wanted a job. I would like to say that I had a desire to work and learn how businesses were ran, but in reality, I just hoped for some extra money to be able to buy the things that I wanted.

At my interview, I remember being asked a series of questions that related to me as a person, not so much my ability to do the job. One question in particular stands out to me to this day. The woman interviewing me asked, "What are the three most important things in your life, please list them in order of greatest importance to least."

I didn't even hesitate when I answered, "God, my family, and school."

When it came down to it, those were the things that I felt were helping to shape me into the person that I wanted to be. After I said it, I wondered if I made a mistake by putting school as last on my list, though in that particular hierarchy it was.

She smiled and said, "Can you come in for training tomorrow?"

I got the job and was excited to work somewhere that I knew would not keep me past 10:00 PM on a school night, and also somewhere that would never ask me to work on a Sunday. The location that I worked at was inside of our mall and the mall closed at 9:00 PM each night, so there was no risk of me being there too late. There were a few times that I did have to come to the mall on a Sunday for meetings, usually when the whole staff was scolded for doing something wrong.

It was a pretty intense place to work. My co-workers were nice for the most part, but they took their jobs so seriously that there was never any time to talk to them and get to know anyone. I took my job seriously too, and though I wanted to run a cash register, I ended up having the position of cleaning the dining area.

Let me make one thing clear... I DO NOT LIKE TO CLEAN. I have never enjoyed cleaning, especially other people's messes, but I do a good job at it, so I tended to get put in those positions. I was only a teenager myself, but I would get so angry at the teens who would leave behind messes or purposely create them. One lovely evening, while cleaning the toilets in the cramped bathroom, I noticed something red oozing from beneath the toilet seat.

I lifted the toilet seat and saw that ketchup was all over the place and that four ketchup packets were lining the rim of the toilet. I quickly discovered that a favorite prank of some of the teenagers was to put ketchup packets under the toilet seat lid and when unsuspecting customers would sit on it, they would explode underneath their weight. Sometimes I was able to throw away the packets before anyone had a chance to sit on them, but it all came down to timing. I couldn't monitor the bathroom my entire shift when there were condiments to straighten, tables to wipe, and floors to clean.

It was grueling work, and had I not been working with the goal of buying a MacBook Pro that would hopefully get me through my years in college, then I probably would have quit sooner. One evening, a woman was standing in line holding her child. Nothing seemed out of the ordinary until the child opened its mouth and shot out a waterfall of vomit. To this day, I am amazed at how much liquid came out of that tiny child when it threw up.

I just watched in awe, knowing that any moment the shift

manager would come rushing over to me requesting that I clean it. One of the custodial staff at the mall was nearby and let out a sigh.

"You've got to be kidding me. It's on our side..." He said.

I wasn't sure what he meant until he explained that the projectile vomit had flew so far from the kid that it was technically outside of Chick-Fil-A and part of the area that was cleaned by the mall custodial staff. I was so thankful that I wouldn't be the one who had to clean up that mess. The woman turned and advanced in the line to order her food as if nothing had happened, as if this were just something that kids do all the time. She never even apologized or thanked the custodian that spend half an hour scooping up slippery chunks of her kid's stomach juices.

Parents sometimes apologize when their children do things at stores to make the employee's lives more difficult, though often times they do not. It is assumed that because you are getting paid to be there, you shouldn't mind doing anything that is asked of you. I am here to say that it is terrible to be treated like you are less than someone else because you have a job. If you are one of the people who view employees of a business as lesser beings than yourself, then please take a step back and consider that you are being rude to someone's child, a person that might someday be an astronaut or a doctor.

I never went on to build rockets or anything like that, but I have gone on to work in education and still experience the thanklessness of the public, perhaps more now than I did then. I have never needed an award for doing a job, but neutrality would be preferable to how most people act towards employees. When I see someone that looks sad handing food out of a drive-thru window, I say a little prayer for them because I know what they are going through.

After working about six months at Chick-Fil-A, it was time for me to spread my chicken wings and fly the coop. I had hoped that my next job would be in retail. Mentally, I was finished working in fast-food. One day, I got a call for an interview at K-Mart, then Sears, and it seemed like I had a chance at doing something other than cleaning and being surrounded by chicken grease. My interview at Sears went well, but they told me I was really too young for the job and the interview at K-Mart was a dismal failure.

When asked why I wanted to be a cashier, I responded by saying, "I'm really good at it and it is something that I actually enjoy doing." The manager interviewing me started laughing. My face was serious, but he seemed to think that I was joking. No, being a cashier wasn't my dream job, but it was something that I had done a few times at Chick-Fil-A and I found that I was very good at and knew I would enjoy doing it on a regular basis, especially in comparison to the other jobs that most places were hiring for.

I left that interview walking slowly down the gray isles, fluorescent lights flickering overhead, knowing that I didn't get the job. My next job actually ended up being at McDonalds. I had expected it to be similar to Chick-Fil-A in terms of the work atmosphere, but it was something entirely different.

I was only allowed to work a certain number of hours as a part-time employee, but in reality I think they would have let me live there if I never asked to clock-out and go home.

I worked more hours in my three months at McDonalds than I ever would have thought possible. When I think back to that period of time in my life, all I can remember is going in to work, always working more than my scheduled shift, and going home long enough to sleep and come back the next day to do it all again. At the time, they were open 24-hours a day, seven days a week, with the exception of the dining room closing at around 10:00 PM. Luckily, I had my drivers license by then and working longer hours wasn't such an issue.

Around ninety percent of the time I was able to work at the cash register, while the other ten percent of the time I was making fries or cleaning. I actually didn't mind the work that I did there too much, and my co-workers loved to talk, so the summer seemed to go by quickly. I also really liked that they gave us our paychecks each week, whereas almost everywhere else paid every two weeks.

One evening while working the cash register, I heard a loud scream come from the kitchen. I thought that someone had either burned themselves on the grill or gotten cut with a knife.

"One moment." I told the customer as I prepared to rush back to the kitchen and see what had happened.

"What's going on?" I asked.

The shift manager was standing before a large stack of

trays that contained hamburger buns. One of the trays was on the floor, the buns scattered on the brown tiles from the force of being hastily dropped.

"There's a dead rat in the hamburger buns." She said, pointing to one of the trays of buns. Placed on the tray among the golden bread was a smashed rat. It was flat looking, so my guess is that it was crushed when someone at the bread factory was loading the trays onto a truck.

"What do we do?" I asked.

"Don't say anything...just go back out there and take the customer's orders like normal. I will get rid of this entire shipment of buns and get some fresh ones in here." She said.

True to her word, she removed all of the trays of buns that had been in that lot and got some fresh ones brought in, sanitizing every area that the bun trays had been in previously. This wasn't anything that could have been avoided on the part of McDonald's, perhaps the bread factory could have discovered this sooner, but I have learned that in the fast-food industry there are always little critters waiting around for their next chance at getting something to eat. Perhaps that rat had dreams of tasting the secret Big Mac sauce, or perhaps it was just in the wrong place at the wrong time. Either way, I think the shift manager handled the situation pretty well, shouting aside.

After three months I got a call from Kroger, a grocery store about a ten-minute drive from my house. The idea of working somewhere other than fast-food and shortening my drive by about eight minutes was too much to resist. I took the job as "bag boy" and prepared for my exciting new job bagging groceries. In retrospect, I should have stayed at McDonald's because Kroger ended up being a depressing job. I was miserable, and I think it had a lot to do with the excess of rude customers and sterile atmosphere of the store. It was like the second I walked through the automatic doors, all joy and happiness was sucked out of the air.

One night, a customer came in and dropped a large bottle of alcohol. Judging by the way that they stumbled out of the store, leaving their mess behind without so much as a "sorry", they were probably already drunk.

"Clean it up." Demanded the shift manager.

I did as I was instructed, no mall custodians around to help me that time. It got to a point where I had to actively tell myself each day that I went into work that I wouldn't have to work there forever. The reason that I was working there was to save money for college so that I wouldn't have to work at jobs that I hated doing. I would try and busy my mind by making up stories as I collected the shopping carts from the parking lot. We were studying poetry in my English class at school, Emily Dickinson in particular, so I would write short poems in my head to help pass the time.

Here is one of the poems that I wrote on the spot during class, followed by one that I wrote while collecting shopping carts. The atmospheric tone of both are in line with words that I feel Emily Dickinson would appreciate.

If to be murdered by a blanket of silence
The world would go away
Leave me to my thoughts
Then I'd have lived for just one day

∼

The irrational thoughts
Of a rational man
Are thoughts that will never be known
For a rational man
Who thinks these thoughts
Will always be alone

∼

LIKE I SAID, not the most upbeat poetry, but if I had to pick a color to describe that period in my life, I would choose gray. Having a job that you dread going to can really affect everything else in life. I try to keep this in mind when I talk to someone and they tell me they don't like their job. Normally, it is because of circumstances that could be remedied if everyone else at their job got together and decided to make changes.

You think your job is depressing? Everyone could try and make it a joyful place by having small celebrations or getting to know one another a bit better. Not sure why customers keep treating you like you are less than human? The store could make a policy where their employees do not have to tolerate being spoken down to and politely remind customers of this when situations start to go bad. There are a lot of little things that businesses could do to make the work life of their employees not only bearable but enjoyable.

My friend called me one day and asked if I would be able to come in and help them make ice-cream cones. She worked at Sonic Drive-In and loved her job.

"We can pay you and everything, but we just don't have enough employees." She said, her panicked tone evident.

It was the evening of my graduation party and my family was in from out of state, so I hated to tell them that I had to go, but luckily the party was dwindling to a close and they were staying a few days and didn't mind. As soon as I got to Sonic, they started giving me a crash course in how to make milkshakes, slushes, and ice-cream cones. In about ten minutes, I had all of the information I would need to help for the rest of the evening.

It was extremely fast-paced, but my friend was right, it was fun. I don't know if the tasks of the job itself were what I enjoyed, or if it was just being able to work with one of my friends. That evening flew by and the manager was impressed with the work that I had done.

"You wouldn't want to work here, would you?" He asked.

I didn't even hesitate when I told him, "Yes."

When I left Kroger, I already had the job at Sonic, so I did not feel like I was leaving any opportunities behind there. My drive to Sonic would be double or more what it was to

Kroger, but I knew that I would enjoy the work and being around the people that I worked with. The atmosphere was great, it was like meeting up with friends every evening to make desserts for people.

One day my friend was eating the cherries that we used to top desserts with. There was a large jar that was filled with them and she asked if I wanted some. We ate so many that I felt sick. The shift managers there were very relaxed, perhaps too relaxed, and encouraged us to enjoy the little perks of our job.

The shift manager's boyfriend worked there as the cook and he was also a really chill person, so chill that he would end up falling asleep on the job...a lot. There were many times where I ended up doing the job of the cook because he had fallen asleep somewhere. One evening, he was missing and everyone assumed that he was outside of the building somewhere, but when I went to get a sleeve of Styrofoam cups I found him asleep on the floor, inside of the cup box.

The store did amazing business and while it was an extremely fun place to work during the few months between graduating high school and getting ready for my first year of college, I only stayed a few months. Shortly after I left the place, it ended up shutting down due to multiple failed health inspections and mismanagement. They definitely did not hold their employees to the same standards that Chick-Fil-A did, or even the same standards as McDonald's for that matter.

I have had many jobs since, but these are the ones that I had while in high school. I look at this as a time when I learned a lot about the jobs that so many people do to keep the world going, the jobs that I had to do myself. It made me appreciate those who work for minimum wage and realize that those working for the minimum are often times the ones who do the most. I have a deep respect for every person in every field of work because I learned during that time that no job, no matter how small, is unimportant. So, the next time you order from a restaurant, or purchase something at a grocery store, think about the people around you wearing the employee uniforms and how each of them has a life of their own. Give someone a random compliment. Ask them how their day is going. You never know how important showing a little human kindness can be.

30

FALL FESTIVAL

The PTO at my school held events every so often to raise funds for specific groups. One fundraiser that they did often in elementary school was a gospel singing to help fund the Bible In The Schools program. When I got to high school, the events that they would hold were a bit different; one such event was the Fall Festival.

My Nanny took my brother and I to the event. They were going to hold a silent auction for some items to raise funds, have games that you could buy tickets to play and win prizes, and even have a haunted house type of attraction. They had apparently purchased way too many prizes because any time that you won a game, you ended up with a ton of really cool things.

I remember winning ink pens that looked like syringes filled with blood, pencils, erasers, notepads, plastic spiders and skeletons, and of course vampire fangs. There were a lot of standard Halloween trinkets and candy which made for a really fun time. Though most of the evening was spent playing games, I do remember a few other unique things that were offered.

I spent some of my tickets to see the terrifying Halloween show that they were building up hype for by creating a false sense of horror. Students would leave the JROTC room where the movie was being shown, screaming and looking terrified. The movie, which only lasted about four minutes, cost way more tickets than any of the other things you could spend them on. I decided that it was worth it, so I paid my tickets and went in to watch the "movie".

My heart was racing with anticipation of the terrifying things that I was about to see. When the room was filled, they started the film. What proceeded to play was scary and not because of the content, but because of the fact that I had spent a large quantity of my tickets to see it. The "Thriller" music video by Michael Jackson played on the projector screen and while the music video is a classic, my hopes of seeing something truly terrifying had been built up and knocked down.

When the video was over the adult that was overseeing that room of the Fall Festival said, "Now we need to make this seem really scary. On the count of three I need everyone to scream as loud as you possibly can. One... Two... Three!"

Everyone in the room, except for me, was screaming as if they had just witnessed the most frightening thing they had ever seen. My ears were hurting from the shrill cries of the other students.

"Great job! Now when you leave the room, make sure you look scared. If anyone asks you about the movie, just tell them that you can't talk about it because it was so scary, and mention that they will just have to come see it for themselves." The adult instructed us.

I couldn't help but be impressed by this genius marketing move. Think about it, nobody can stay mad for too long when you get to see the "Thriller" music video on a big screen at a Fall Festival, and they are bringing the audience in on the secret by having you scream at the end and look afraid. The line for that room was the longest out of any of them throughout the entire event. It just goes to show that a simple idea can have impressive results if it is marketed well.

It was fun getting to see how my school looked after normal operating hours. Fall Festivals tend to work well at schools because of the following reasons:

- You already have an audience that will attend your event and bring their family along.
- Everyone knows where the event is taking place…hopefully.
- People don't mind paying money if they know it is going towards something education related.
- The parents who don't want to attend like the idea of dropping off their kids for an evening of peace and quiet at home.

- Schools are just plain creepy after-hours.

While in college, I was asked to work at a Fall Festival at an elementary school near my university. I was able to earn volunteer hours for the program that I was a part of, so I decided that I would do it. I can say that it is not nearly as much fun working at a Fall Festival as it is to attend one. Things don't look quite as amazing from behind-the-scenes.

At that particular festival, I was in charge of a game where students would reach into a box of keys and try to find the one that would unlock the lock attached to a prize box. It was a really unique concept and one that the students loved. That game ended up being pretty popular among the seven and eight-year-olds, though it got old for me pretty quickly. Try acting like the game you are in charge of is the most amazing one at the festival and doing that for an entire evening and tell me you wouldn't get tired of it by the time each kid was on their thirtieth try at unlocking the box.

If you plan on hosting a Fall Festival and offering this game, take a little piece of advice from me and don't put fifty different keys in the box. Offer the player of the game a few key choices, ten at the most, and only give them a few guesses as to which key is the correct one. Otherwise, the person in charge of that game will have to spend half an hour on each kid's turn, and that's not fun for anyone.

31

ALL THAT I WANT

Have you ever heard a song that stands out so much that you can't get it out of your head? I often face the experience of hearing such songs and then fearing that I will never know the name of the song and lose it forever. Such was the music that filled my teenage years. I discovered some of my all-time favorite songs during that time in my life.

I was not interested in many of the songs that topped the charts. Don't get me wrong, I would listen to a catchy song no matter how popular it was, but I tended to play the more independent songs on repeat. Many of the songs that filled my Apple iPod Touch as a teenager, not the iPod Nano that I cherished for many years previously, were songs that I had discovered from television commercials.

This was a time period when commercials were not only

accentuated by how good the song used was, but they were based on it. I can remember certain commercials solely because of the song that they had chosen the play during their short thirty second run. I remember discovering Lenka because of an Ugly Betty commercial featuring the song "The Show" that was played during every ad break on ABC.

One evening, around Christmas time, I saw a commercial for JCPenney that featured a simple song that I couldn't get out of my head. I quickly committed a few of the lyrics to memory, ran to my computer to type them in, and hoped for an accurate result. Sometimes I would end up spending hours searching for a specific song, never finding the correct one.

The result was almost instant as the commercial had caught the attention of the internet. The song was called "All That I Want" and was by a band called The Weepies. I spent the rest of that evening listening to their other songs and falling in love with the words that they used. The music was brilliant in its own right, but the lyrics to their songs were so simple and true, unlike anything else that I had ever heard before.

Now, if you're starting to think that it was weird to look up songs based on a few lyrics you caught in a commercial, you are mistaken. There were, and probably still are, entire websites dedicated to people trying to find a particular song that they are in search of. Some of the websites even go so far as to have entire communities that will help you search for a song if you provide them with a few lyrics.

Searching for some songs with very little information to go on is similar to when someone goes to a bookstore and says they are looking for a book but the only information that they have is that it had a red cover. Having worked in a bookstore before, this is much more common than you might think. It is like the feeling that you get when you forget what you are about to say, a nagging sensation that bothers you.

If it had not been for that JCPenney commercial, I might have never discovered The Weepies and filled so many of my teenage years with their music. They didn't release music as often as some bands, but when they did it was music worth listening to. I knew all of their lyrics by heart and within moments of one of their songs coming on the radio or starting to be played in a department store I could tell you the name of the song.

The Weepies were a husband-and-wife duo that wrote and performed original music. They would also create artwork for their album covers and promotional materials. If I had to choose one band to call my favorite, it would be them. I am not sure that I will ever change my mind because as I grow older; their music seems to grow with me.

They announced on their Facebook page that they would be going on tour. I am sure that they had toured plenty in the past, but that was before I knew about them. Finding out that they would be traveling the country and performing was exciting enough, but when one of the venue locations announced was in West Virginia, I couldn't believe it. I had commented to them once before that if they went on tour they should come to West Virginia and I like to think that this is the reason they to come here on one of their stops. Though I have no proof other than my comment to prove this, there is no evidence to the contrary.

I told my parents and they didn't hesitate to tell me that we could go. They knew how important this band was to me and I think they were a little surprised too when I mentioned that they were coming to West Virginia. They would be playing at Mountain Stage in Charleston, the state capitol, along with a few other bands that I wasn't too concerned with. The other bands were The Infamous String Dusters, Trampled by Turtles, and the Punch Brothers. The only ones I had ever listened to were The Weepies.

I had been doing small paintings on blocks of wood of their album covers for a while. My parents and my brother would be attending the concert with me and they suggested that I take two of the wood paintings to give to them at the show. As we waited in line for the doors to the auditorium to open, the person running their merchandise booth asked if I was a fan of The Weepies. She must have been able to tell when I bought a ton of their merch, so I told her that I was and that I wanted to give them the paintings that I had done.

She was impressed at how accurate they were to their album designs and said that I couldn't give them to them personally, but that she would be sure that they received them if I left them with her. I didn't really want to hold the paintings throughout the show, though they were no bigger than a square paperback book, so I gave them to her. I sent them a Tweet after the show to ask if they got them and never heard back. To this day I don't know if they ever got them.

I was pleasantly surprised that this was the type of show where you could sit. It was more of a theater stage than a concert hall and it was awesome not having to stand the entire night. The other bands were clearly talented too, but the type of music they played was much more fast paced than what The Weepies performed. Trampled by Turtles was honestly pretty intense and probably the closest thing to a rock band you will find in the folk category.

When it was time for The Weepies to perform, my Dad turned on the flip video camera that we had brought with us and filmed the entire thing for me. His arm must have been ridiculously tired from holding still the entire time that they performed, but he knew how important that moment was for me. They performed on the Mountain Stage, a pretty upscale venue located on the grounds of the state capitol, and even talked about how it had always been one of their goals to play there.

I don't think that going to see them in-person would have been as impactful of an event in my life as it was if my family wasn't there with me. None of them were fans like I was, they didn't dislike their music, but they wouldn't have chosen to drive that far to see them if it weren't for me wanting to. I think that I will always remember that evening at the Mountain Stage, the feeling that my family was there not for the music but for me, and knowing that it never would have happened if I had not heard the words calling from the television, "All that I want."

32

ATLANTA

Having grown up in the mountains, I wasn't sure when I would ever visit a real city. I had always assumed that I would go to New York someday and that would be my first trip to a big city. We had smaller cities around, but the idea of going somewhere so large that the buildings overhead could block out the sky was one that kept me imagining what those places would be like.

My tenth-grade year of high school a program called Greater Appalachian Outreach offered to take students that qualified on a trip to Atlanta, Georgia. One of the ways that you could qualify for the trip was to have a family that had not ever attended a college or university. I think the idea was to inspire us to go to college after we graduated. I already had plans of going to college to become a teacher, but finding out that I qualified for this trip almost seemed too good to be true.

They were going to pay for all of our transportation costs, hotels, food, and tickets to the attractions that we were going to visit. I told my parents about it and they happily agreed to let me go. Atlanta was far from my home in West Virginia, and the few days that the trip lasted would be the longest amount of time that I would have ever been away from my parents. Of course, my parents were worried about my safety, but they knew how big of an opportunity this was and wanted me to enjoy it.

There were quite a few students that qualified to go, enough that we were able to fill a charter bus. On the day that we were to leave, my parents drove me to the school, and we said goodbye as I boarded the bus. The drive to Atlanta was a long one lasting over seven hours, but we left late in the evening and were able to sleep on the way there overnight. I discovered that it is nearly impossible for me to get comfortable enough on a charter bus to sleep. While most everyone else seemed to have no problems getting dozing off, I struggled and got only about two hours of sleep.

During one of my short bouts of sleep I felt the bus stop. I opened my eyes, and we were in the parking lot of a budget motel. The bus driver got off and someone came out of one of the rooms. They talked for a moment and then the person who had stepped out of the room got on the bus and we continued with him as our bus driver. They had swapped, our previous driver presumably going to sleep in the motel room while the person who was fully rested took their place. I later learned that this is common with some tour bus companies as it allows their drivers to work more in the long run without getting exhausted.

When the sun started to shine through the windows, everyone else began to yawn and make shuffling sounds of waking up. I believe we had some type of prepackaged breakfast, a granola bar or something, but we didn't stop the rest of the way to Atlanta. One of the students was talking about how they could watch videos on their new phone. As they showed off how fast it would load the video clips, I watched in amazement.

These were the very early days of having data on a cell phone. At the time I had a Razr flip-phone and was pretty happy with it. Pretty much everyone else that I knew had flip-phones too. You could get data on the phones, but it was very expensive and there wasn't much that you would be able to do even if you had it. But the technology running that student's phone was called 3G and it is crazy fast. If I want to listen to a song, it could have it loaded on here in about half a minute.

"We're only about thirty minutes outside of the city." The group leader told us.

I got out my Razr phone and started typing a text to my parents to let them know that we were almost there. I was pretty quick at typing out a text message using a numeric keypad; almost everyone I knew was. My Nanny had even started to learn how to text this way. Having a full keyboard with the alphabet on it was a luxury and was not standard at the time.

"Almost there, about 30 minutes away from the city." I texted.

When I looked out my window, I noticed that somehow the few lanes of traffic that we had been in were now multiple lanes and I could not believe how many cars were on the road. I have since been to Paris, France and can say that the traffic in Atlanta has nothing on the city of Paris where motorbikes weave in and out of traffic and there seems to be an "anything goes" type of attitude towards driving. There were a few large bridges and the thing that I remember the most about them was all of the homeless people underneath.

I had imagined that Atlanta was a big and bright city filled with prosperous individuals, yet the first thing that you are greeted with before entering the city are the masses of homeless people. I said a silent prayer for them, that God would help them through whatever they were dealing with and that if they hadn't already found him that they would. It broke my heart to see people like that, and it hurt even more to think that they had perhaps lost hope due to their situation. Here we were, a bunch of high school students on a charter bus, admiring a classmate's phone that featured the new "3G" data option, and outside the bus mere feet away were more homeless individuals than I had ever seen in my life.

In the time since that trip, I have learned a lot about homelessness and the issues surrounding it. I have even gotten the opportunity to work directly with those effected and try to play my role in fixing the problem. The problem is rarely the person that is homeless, as I have learned there are more ways than you might think to end up without a home. The image of those people, those precious lives, degraded to living under a bridge to claim some small amount of shelter, has stuck with me all of these years.

The ride to our hotel took longer than I had anticipated. I assumed that once you were in the city, it would be pretty quick to get to where you needed to go. Something else that I have learned since that trip is that more often than not, walking and taking the subway (or metro) when available is the best option. We were staying at the Sheraton and until then I had never even heard of that hotel brand . I would be rooming with two twins that I had never really met before but who seemed nice enough.

"There's a Starbucks on the fourth floor." One of them said to me as we were handed our room card-keys.

"That's awesome!" I replied.

"Yeah, if you like coffee." The other twin said.

It just so happened that I did like coffee. I intended to visit that Starbucks at some point during our trip, but when I eventually did get the chance to go, it was closed. Upon entering our room, I was amazed at the flat screen television. Flat screens were not standard in most hotels at the time, and though I didn't plan on watching it at all during the trip, it was nice to have it to look at. The view from our room was fantastic and the furnishings were more modern than anywhere I had previously stayed.

One of the twins went into the bathroom, shut the door, did what they needed to do, flushed the toilet, and then came back into the room.

"You may want to wait a minute before going in there." He said with a grin.

I was inwardly cringing that he was so blunt about just having used the bathroom. I nodded, making a mental note to try and use the bathroom wherever we went next if I could. The other twin went right in and I noticed something about both of them, they didn't wash their hands. Yes, they were friendly, but they were also disgusting. My roommates were twins who thought that stinking up the bathroom and not washing their hands was normal.

I tried not to focus on the fact that a pair of possums digging through the garbage outside of a truck stop might be cleaner than these two.

"I'm going to head on down to the lobby. We're supposed to meet there in fifteen minutes anyway." I told them.

They nodded and jumped on their bed. Thankfully, they were planning to share a bed and leave me with the other all to myself. I don't think I could have made it if they didn't.

When I got to the lobby, I met up with some of my friends and we waited for our group leader to arrive so that we could reembark on the bus and start touring. There was a roped off area in the lobby that was used to showcase what the rooms looked like inside. There was a bed along with everything else you would find in your room, all on display. I thought this was strange but decided that maybe it was just something that expensive hotels did. For the record, I have never been to another hotel that does this, and I have stayed in some pretty nice ones, this was just a weird thing that was being done at that particular hotel.

The first place that we toured was the National Weather Service. The building was pretty far outside of the city and I was actually very disappointed that we were touring anything that wasn't surrounded by other buildings. The structure was old and gave off the same vibe that a doctor's office from the 1970's might. Even the technology that they were using seemed outdated to me. Giant cream-colored computer monitors were on just about every desk and hulking towers sat on the floor. I had been to the Clay Center in Charleston, West Virginia before, and they had an exhibit where you could pretend to be on television telling about the weather using a green-screen; that technology seemed more powerful than what they were using at the National Weather Service.

I realize now that some of the large computers that they were using at the time were pretty necessary since they offered extremely accurate weather forecasting. As a teenager, I wasn't impressed and couldn't wait until we left. The area surrounding the building resembled a swamp and I worried that we would go deeper into this part of Georgia instead of touring in the city.

Our next stop was the Atlanta Aquarium, which was impressive in design, but not so much in content. There were only a few exhibits that you could visit, and the crowds were so massive that it took a long time just to get close enough to view anything. They did have an impressive room where you could see giant sharks swimming while you stood before the largest screen of glass that I had ever seen. I liked this room because, no matter how crowded it was, everyone could get a good look at the sharks as they calmly swam by.

One thing that stood out to me about the city of Atlanta was how clean and tidy the areas that we visited were. I knew from the scenes under the bridges that there was much more to the city than we were being shown, but the tourist areas were spotless. I have been to cities, New York comes to mind, where even the tourist areas are not very well kept.

My favorite place that we visited was the Coca-Cola Factory. When they told us we would be visiting a factory, I was disappointed as that didn't sound like very much fun. We had already learned about weather services for what felt like hours, and now we were being told we would tour a factory, so I was not looking forward to it. However, once we got there I was completely amazed. The World of Coca-Cola is not like the factories that you might be thinking of, it is almost like a theme park minus the rides.

There was a giant Coca-Cola bear dancing around, a movie that opens up onto the entrance of the attraction, and so many fun activities to experience. My favorite part of the tour was getting to try as many different flavors of Coke products from around the world that I wanted. They give you a small cup and let you taste test as many different drinks as you can handle. Some of them were amazing while others were so bad I wanted to spit them out, though I drank them all anyway. My absolute favorite drink was one from South Africa called Bibo. It was a fruit juice flavored soda and I have not tasted anything like it since then.

To end our tour, we went to Stone Mountain, where we were going to watch a light show displayed on the mountain side. We were instructed to sit on the lawn where we had an amazing clear view of the mountain. The sun was setting, and it wouldn't be long before it was dark enough for the light show to begin. I have had similar experiences at drive-in theaters where you arrive and wait for it to get dark enough for the movie to start. It is a fun concept to let the sun dictate when you are able to view something and I think that is part of the experience.

Since we still had some time before it would be dark enough for the laser light show to begin, I decided to go to the gift shop anyway and buy some souvenirs. When no one was looking I went to the gift shop, which was only about a hundred feet away from where we were told to sit, and I went inside quickly, choosing gifts that I would take back home to my parents and grandparents. They had given me money to buy souvenirs and I always made it a point to spend any money that I was given on school trips.

I got a really cool mug that had a 3D feel to it where certain parts were raised to emphasize an element of the design and my parents still have it to this day. The shop was closing pretty soon so I made it a point to get whatever I could find, rush to the checkout, and pay for everything. I left with a large bag filled with souvenirs and when our group leader saw me, she wasn't too happy.

"I was looking for you. We did a head count, and you were missing." She said.

"I'm sorry, I just wanted to get some souvenirs." I replied, a smile on my face.

"Go sit with everyone else." She said with a sigh of both frustration and relief.

I couldn't believe that I hadn't gotten in trouble! There was really no danger to worry about as my group was not far away from the gift shop and I had my cell phone with me, but in retrospect, I would have been much more upset if a student I had taken on an out-of-state trip did something like this. I admit that I was naïve about the world and thought that everyone was simply good. It was nice not knowing about all of the ways that going off on my own could have gone wrong. Though I had been warned to stay safe ever since I could remember, I made a decision that luckily ended up working out.

We watched the light show and I filmed the entire thing on my digital camera. There wouldn't have been any point trying to get photos or video of it on my Razr because I don't think it even had a one-megapixel camera on it. I made so many good memories on that trip.

I learned that cities are not like they appear on television and in the movies, unless we are talking about Paris, in which case it is even better in person in my opinion. I learned that not everyone is fortunate enough to see a city from the perspective of a tourist. I learned that I can room with twins that have very poor personal hygiene if it means I get to see a whale shark. Lastly, I learned that sneaking off to buy souvenirs, no matter how badly you want them, is not a wise thing to do…unless were talking about a 3D coffee mug.

33

VAMPIRES

I decided to join the drama club my tenth-grade year of high school. I didn't really participate much in after-school activities. I was happy just to go home and relax after a day of school, but I had taken a class with the teacher over the drama club, and she really sold it to all of us as an amazing experience. The students in the club were very over-the-top in personality and didn't seem to mind getting up and performing on a stage.

My personality didn't particular fit that profile, but the teacher insisted that I audition for one of the main roles in the upcoming play, *Dracula*. She thought that I would be perfect for the role of Mina Harker's Father, Doctor Seward. I was to be one of the characters that had a presence throughout the play and quite a bit of dialogue as well. I didn't want to play Dracula because I knew that I didn't want to be the star of the show. I auditioned for the part and she was overjoyed, thinking that I had done a brilliant job.

It sounded like the perfect play to perform with the overly dramatic group of students in the club. Practices were a few times each week after school. They normally lasted about an hour or two. More than half of that time was always spent just talking or listening to the drama teacher stressing over a single thing that someone was doing wrong and that would need to be addressed, otherwise the entire play would be a failure.

Dracula is a pretty intimidating script, especially if you are asked to perform the original, unmodified version that does not fit standards of today's dialogue. We spent an entire practice one evening going over the same few lines until everyone got it right.

"They were inseparable..." I would say about Lucy and Mina.

It was strange for me to talk about fictional characters as if they were real, but I learned that acting is taking on the role of someone else entirely. We were going to go shop for costumes one evening with our teacher. I had never been in drama club before, so I wasn't sure how common this was. In the movies and on television there were always amazing costumes. Our reality was that the club had very little funding to work with and we needed to find ways to get our own costumes.

I was happy to learn that mine would simply be a labcoat since I was to play the role of a doctor. We spent that evening at a local thrift store, I mostly stood around and talked because I already had my costume, and then everyone went to Burger King afterward. My teacher bought me a large chicken-fry and drink (this was a time period when I was not yet a vegetarian).

The teacher over drama club was super nice and she really seemed to love what she taught. It is unfortunate that we never got to perform the play *Dracula*. As the date was nearing for our small production, it was discovered that many of the students playing leading roles did not know but a fraction of their lines. If we had performed the play it would have been a disaster. It turns out that spending the majority of each practice talking and having fun didn't make for a professional production-ready play.

There was talk about postponing it to the next year, but the disappointment led to many of the members of the club leaving, including me. While I never did get to perform as the doctor in *Dracula*, I had fun at my attempt of being a part of an after-school club. In the end, when I looked at my role in the club, I knew that I was not dedicated to my role enough to spending another year practicing the same lines. I didn't want to be a doctor for another year in the hopes of having my on-stage dialogue heard by the ears of my classmates, who more than likely would have difficult following the events of the play anyway.

I have always enjoyed the concept of vampires, so it is unfortunate that the play never happened. Even without me and a few of the others, the drama club tossed out *Dracula* and instead performed *A Midsummer Night's Dream*. They did a fantastic job with it and the audience found it funny, even though the words were not modern, the concepts still seemed to be.

Years later, I would go on to write a book about a family of vampires. The concept would be based on the idea that a family of vampires owned a funeral home. That book would end up being rewritten in an entirely different point-of-view, turned into a series of books, and go on to be one of my most cherished writing projects. You get to know the characters that you write about as if they were real, and in many ways they are. Just like acting, writing a story requires you to accept the lives of fictional characters as being reality.

Though no vampires graced the stage at my high school, I still have memories of our practices and my attempt at joining a club. It is hard to say what moments from that time in my life influenced the decision to write a series of books about vampires later on. Who knows? Maybe some day in the future *Dracula* will be performed on that stage, hopefully with a cast that can memorize their lines well.

34

NOT ONLY FOR THE OLD

Every time that I would go to the doctor, or the dentist, or the optometrist I would expect to get a similar response.

"That's strange. This is normally seen in the elderly." They would say.

The first time that I heard this was when I went to the eye doctor over an issue that had started to occur. My tenth-grade year in school I was sitting in art class and then all of the sudden I saw a gray flashing spot in my vision. I was familiar with the random spots that would sometimes appear, but they always seemed to go away shortly after.

When the gray spot didn't go away and I started to worry that it would be permanent, I went to see the eye doctor. He examined my eyes and viewed them with a microscope that projected an image of what was in my eye onto an old television screen. My mom was with me and when she saw the image on the screen, she couldn't believe it.

"You have what is called asteroid hyalosis. We normally only see this in the elderly and in animals." He informed us.

I was not sure how to respond to that news.

"Is it permanent, is there a cure?" My Mom asked.

My mom has dealt with vision problems since she was young, so she understood how devastating this news could be.

"There isn't a cure, but I'm not a specialist either. There isn't anything that can be done about it, but it shouldn't really affect his vision. It's frustrating, but that's about it."

"So, he just has to live with it?" She asked again.

"I can refer you to a specialist out-of-state, but they will tell you the same thing that I'm telling you."

He was an excellent doctor and I had been going to see him since I was very young, so we trusted his judgement, no matter how much we didn't like the news. On top of the asteroid hyalosis, I also had floaters that were pretty annoying.

Over the years that gray spot that wasn't supposed to affect my vision has turned into a blind spot. Though I don't pay any attention to it and have gotten used to not seeing in that area, it is frustrating that there was never really any reason as to why I had it. That eye doctor has since retired, and I have been to see others that tell me similar things.

Over the years it has caused me a lot of grief and trouble, but in the past few years it has gotten to the point that it is almost non-existent. I believe a lot of it had to do with my diet and bad lifestyle choices. I have never been very proactive in making healthy choices, but lately I have realized how important that can be to every aspect of your life.

The next time that I heard this was when I went to the doctor over a rash that had appeared on the left side of my stomach. I assumed that it was just a regular rash that would go away after a few days, though I had never had one there before. I went in to work and noticed how even the slightest brush of my shirt fabric against my skin was painful. It was like a stabbing pain any time that I would breathe.

I was working at Books-A-Millon, and had they known that I wasn't feeling well, they would have gladly let me take the night off, but I didn't tell anyone because I didn't think it was a big deal. I was closing that night, so I got out the heavy vacuum and cleaned the entire store. Thankfully, it was a pretty small store, but it was still about a half-hour of lugging that vacuum around to each of the power outlets stationed at intervals. I wish that they had a cordless vacuum because it would have saved so much time and energy.

I was in immense much pain the next day, so I went to the doctor.

"Lift your shirt and let me see it." The doctor said.

I gently lifted my shirt, taking care not to scrape it against my skin.

He immediately said, "That's shingles."

In a matter of seconds, he knew exactly what it was.

"We don't normally see it in people your age." He said.

I wasn't surprised. I was convinced that I had inherited unhealthy genes from the older generations of my family. While a lot of times that can be the case, I do think that making healthy choices has a lot to do with it. He informed me that he was almost certain that mine had been brought on by stress. I was in college at the time and I cared way more than I should have about making the best grades possible in every single class.

Since then, I have had other health problems directly related to stress. Teaching is a stressful job if you take it seriously and care about what you are doing. I personally do not understand how anyone could be a teacher and say that they don't get stressed on a regular basis. I have had to learn how to manage stress and focus on the important things. While I do still experience stress on occasion, I have come to accept that not everything has to be perfect.

Now, when I go to the doctor, I don't have any expectations. I don't go into the hospital or office with any negative thoughts, but I also don't imagine that there will be excellent news each time either. Someday, they will have to stop telling me, "We normally only see this in the elderly." Until that day I will continue to focus on what matters and try to make healthier choices.

35

VEGETARIAN

One of the questions that I frequently get asked is what made me want to become a vegetarian. It is a very valid question since this is something that has affected the places I can eat and what I am able to eat. There are a few different reasons that I am a vegetarian, but the reason that I became one originally was because of the unnecessary violence towards animals that I saw being committed.

In high school, I knew what a vegetarian was, but I never really saw it as being an option for me. I would tell myself things like, "My family eats too much fast food for me to ever be able to be a vegetarian." I met a friend in my Creative Writing class who told me that she was a vegetarian. She introduced me to PETA, People for the Ethical Treatment of Animals, and the rest was history.

Though I am not a supporter of PETA anymore due to

their extremist ways of protesting, I do have to admit that if it weren't for them, I might not be a vegetarian today. I have been a vegetarian for years and I don't regret a single day of not eating meat. They would send anyone that requested it, supplies and materials on animal cruelty and why you should not eat meat. It was the free stickers that were what drew me in.

It wasn't long before I was helping them with campaigns against dissections in Science class and protesting fur products. The campaigns were usually very fun and targeted at a high school audience. PETA2 was their teen focused group that supplied materials to students.

I did not dissect the fetal pig or frog in Science class because I viewed it as needless. With all of the technology alternatives available, high school students don't need to do a dissection on a dead animal. I have heard arguments that it is good experience in case anyone wants to go on to the medical field after high school, but if that is truly the case then get a fake dead animal that can be reused over and over to provide the same educational value. Get an animal that died of natural causes or something, but why farm these creatures just so they can be killed and played with in a high school class?

My teacher was a very kind person and she paired me with another student who made it clear they were looking forward to the dissection.

"I don't want you to get a bad grade for missing these dissections. It's a large portion of your overall grade. You can just observe your partner doing the discretion and fill out your lab report and still get full credit." She said.

I was lucky, not all teachers would have been so understanding. My partner did indeed enjoy the direction. She would take the tiny scissors and cut little parts of the pig, laughing as she cut off bits and pieces of the dead animal that were not required for the experiment. The other students around me did the same, giggling when they rammed the pointed end of their scalpels into the pig's stomach. It was pretty much what I had expected.

I feel like if you cannot respect the life of an animal, or any living thing for that matter, then you will have a harder time respecting human life. Animal life and human life are two very different things, but if you take pleasure in the fact that something died needlessly for you to play around with its dead body then I believe you will have a harder time respecting life in any form.

There is a quote by Wm. Paul Young from one of his books that sums up my feelings about this situation perfectly. It says, "...if anything matters then everything matters." I believe that to be one of the truths of life. If any life matters, then why shouldn't every life matter?

I watched a few documentaries that showed what actually goes on at slaughterhouses and food production facilities. Aside from the general lack of cleanliness and their disregard for health standards, there was obvious animal abuse and neglect. There was no shortage of stories on animals sitting in their own waste for weeks at a time until some of them died. I saw workers breaking the legs of cows, putting them through unimaginable pain during childbirth. I witnessed baby chickens having their beaks cut off and their necks slit open on an assembly line, tiny creatures begging for their lives as their brothers and sisters fell between cracks or were crushed by conveyor-belts, the modernization of murder.

I wonder how anyone could see where their food comes from and numb themselves enough to be able to ignore all of the facts and continue eating meat. Do you love animals? Then ask yourself how you can support an industry that sees them as nothing more than a pre-packaged product. Cruelty in the meat industry is completely unacceptable and unfortunately widely unregulated. If someone wants to take out their anger on an innocent animal at the factory that they work at, and they happen to mutilate the animals beyond recognition and kill them, there really are no consequences for their actions at the moment.

"It's just an animal." Seems to be the mindset of a lot of the population.

How have we become so accustomed to killing a living creature for a single meal? I ask myself these questions frequently to try and understand why I was ever so complacent in supporting this industry? It all started with me seeing the truth and deciding that I didn't want to be any part of what was going on. I did not want my money going to the corporations that standardize cruelty towards animals.

Over time, I have come to see and feel the physical benefits of not eating meat. When I consumed meat, I had headaches regularly, almost every day. I had grown so accustomed to them that I started to think that it was normal. Once or twice a year, I would have a debilitating migraine that would force me to stay in bed until they would end. These migraines would cause some part of my body to go numb, usually my hand or arm, and I would see flashes of light known as auras followed by incredibly intense pain in my head.

Since I stopped eating meat, I rarely have a headache. I am thankful for this unexpected benefit of not eating meat. When you think about the quality of your food, it doesn't make sense that something's rotting flesh, pumped full of chemicals to keep it fresh, could be transported and sold to you and still be considered healthy. When a body dies, it starts to decompose and rot, and animals are no exception. Thanks to chemicals, the meat is able to stay seemingly "fresh" until you purchase it. It makes me sick to my stomach just thinking about it.

There are so many alternatives in today's world that it is not necessary to consume meat. I often hear that people eat meat because it is good for them or they need protein. This argument is sadly incorrect. Yes, we need protein, but there is protein in just about everything we eat. Your average person can easily get enough protein, possibly without even trying, just by eating a healthy meat-free diet. We are lucky enough to live in an age where we don't have to hunt animals to be able to eat and survive. Most people go to the same grocery stores that I do, but the only difference is they choose to purchase meat whereas I choose not to. It all comes down to making the right decision for yourself and for what you feel is right.

While I am a vegetarian, I respect people's decision not to be. I just ask that everyone take a few moments to actually learn where their food is coming from. If you feel good about eating meat after you see where it comes from, then that is your choice, and you are free to determine that. As for me, I value my health and I don't see how putting something else's dead body into my own could be beneficial. Hopefully this clears up why I decided to become a vegetarian. I do not intend to ever go back to eating meat. This is what I feel to be right for myself and for innocent helpless animals that rely on humans to be their voice. The way I see it, we can speak up for the helpless, or we can contribute our resources towards the problem. I know which option I choose.

36

THE ROOM UPSTAIRS

The go-to for high school students on a weekend seemed to have always been going to the mall. I am not so sure that teenagers go much now, but when I was in high school, it was just about the only thing to do. I spent many Saturday evenings at the mall and movie theater that was located behind it.

A small coffee shop opened one fall season and my friends and I would look forward to going to the mall, getting an overpriced coffee, and walking around. I know, that sounds like a ton of fun, doesn't it? The coffee shop had a clever name, Hebrews Coffee. Do you get it? "He" "Brews" "Coffee"? About this time, there was also a push to have stricter security at the mall, so there was an increase in security guards. I didn't mind this, but I admit that it was a bit unsettling having security guards everywhere, specifically watching every teenager that walked by because you were automatically suspicious if you were that age.

I think that teenagers actually spend quite a bit of money at malls, especially at the one that I was going to. We had our coffees, the kind that are filled with sugar and ice, and my cousin finished drinking his. There was a trash can nearby and he was pretty close to it, so he casually tossed it towards the opening and missed. The empty plastic coffee cup bounced off of the side of the trash can and rolled around on the floor.

My cousin took off running in the opposite direction. One of the newly hired security guards was watching from afar and though we hadn't done anything wrong, I felt guilty just by being there when the trash didn't go directly where it belonged. I picked up his cup and threw it away. We really needed something else to do on the weekends.

I worked off and on during this time, so I didn't have a lot of free time, but when I did, I liked to do normal teenage things. My friend told me about an open mic night where they served amazing food and desserts, so we tried it and that became our new go-to spot to hang out. There was such a mix of age groups at that particular open mic. Everyone from teenagers to the elderly had gathered for the food and entertainment.

They served the biggest slices of cake that I have ever seen. I got them on more than one occasion, along with the other food options, and was never disappointed in the quality of the food. The entertainment was also pretty good as some of the most talented people in the area were going there to perform. It was one of the only places that anyone and everyone was welcome to come and be a part of something based around the local community.

It was a two-floor building, and the second floor was an art gallery. You could hear the music coming from downstairs as you browsed the rotating selection of art by local artist. The bathroom was on the second floor and though it was very small the interior was decorated in an artistic way with blue stained glass windows that would cast a unique light from the moon outside.

The guy who owned the building and set up the open mic events would always talk to my friends and I as if we were adults. He didn't seem to care that we were only teenagers. In fact I believe he saw the artistic potential in young people where others only saw a problem. One evening after the open mic had ended he even asked my friend and I to stay and have some sushi with him and his girlfriend. I declined, but my friend stayed. I probably would have, but alcohol was served at these events and though none of the open mics ever got out of hand, I didn't want to be a teenager amongst a bunch of adults that had been drinking all evening. According to my friend who stayed, it was just more talk of art and of course they had sushi, but nothing bad happened.

Over the years I ended up attending and supporting a lot of the endeavors by the person that funded the open mic events, and though the venue has changed many times, the atmosphere was always the same. It felt like a safe place to spend time with my friends, somewhere that welcomed everyone and showcased the talents of anyone that wanted to perform. When that particular open mic closed down for good, my friends and I started to look for an alternative.

In the neighboring city there was an open mic that we had never been to, but that sounded promising. This particular open mic was being held at a place called "The Room Upstairs". My English teacher had told me that she went there to perform poetry sometimes and hoped to see some of us stop by. Upon arriving at the building where the open mic was taking place, I quickly learned why the venue was given that particular name. In order to get to "The Room Upstairs" you had to go up a narrow set of stairs that seemed to go on forever. At the very top of one of the large buildings downtown was the expansive room where the stage for the open mic was.

I don't think that I ever saw any elderly people at those open mics like I did at the other one and I assume that is because the hike up those stairs would have been too much for them. The talent there was also great. The atmosphere was different but still welcoming. There were large comfortable chairs that you could sit in, a papasan that I claimed more than once, and an open set of windows that gave an excellent view of the street below as the sun would set. It was usually pretty warm, sometimes even hot, because I believe it was an attic space that had been converted into a stage and recording studio. Thankfully, they did eventually get the heating situation fixed.

The first night that my friends and I attended, I lost my iPod Touch that I had taken with me. I called the owners of the open mic when I got home, and they said they found it and would keep it for me until I came back. When I did return to collect my iPod Touch, I spoke with the owners of the business and they were extremely nice. They too appreciated anyone that was interested in the arts. Over the years, I would end up working with them on projects and working for them at the events that they held. That place was also where I formed my online magazine idea with friends once I got to college.

It has been years since I have attended an open mic of any kind, but I highly recommend them for anyone that is looking for a place to share their talent, see local talent, and spend some time with friends. It is also a great place to meet new people and create memories. It sure beats walking around the mall.

37

THE POLICE

I have never personally had any issues involving law enforcement; however, I have been around when some interesting things have happened. My first direct experience with the police was when I was very young. My Nanny and Papaw had taken my brother and I to some type of festival in the city next to ours.

We had enjoyed the day and it was time for us to return home. On our way home there was a police officer stopped at a red light, and wouldn't you know it, we were stopped at the red light too. He waved politely to my brother and I in the back seat. It would have been rude for us not to wave back, at least that was what I thought at the time.

I waved back to the police officer, but I was not very tall, so I worried that he had not seen me. I unbuckled my seatbelt and stood up as much as I could so that he would be able to clearly see me waving back at him. Sometimes, I cannot believe the silly things that I have done. My brother figured that since I was doing it then it must be what he should do too.

When the police officer looked back to our car, he saw two small children, not in seat-belts, waving. I think he even did a double-take because he couldn't believe his eyes. He quickly turned his lights on and pulled my Nanny and Papaw over. They were shocked because they always made sure that we were securely buckled in before starting the car.

"Are you aware that those children are not wearing seat-belts." He asked seriously.

I was confused because he clearly saw that we had previously been wearing seat-belts. I was worried that he was going to arrest them because of something that I had done. Of course, they were not aware that I had unbuckled myself to wave at a police officer. Who would think that their grandchild was that careless?

The police office seemed to understand the situation, though I could tell by the tone in his voice that he blamed them for what my brother and I had done. He warned them about it, saw to it that we were wearing our seat-belts before leaving, and that was the end of that. I truly felt like it was the police officer's fault for waving at me because if he hadn't waved then I never would have unbuckled myself.

The next time that I was around when there was a police officer present was more nerve-racking. My friends had asked me to go with them out of town to eat at Logan's Roadhouse. I had never eaten there before, so I said that I would go. One of my friends was driving, his girlfriend in the passenger seat, and my other friend in the backseat with me.

When we arrived, I was surprised at how freely people were spitting peanut shells onto the floor. I doubt that I would have gone if I knew that I would be walking on an inch-thick layer of peanut shells to get to and from our table. The place was unsettling for someone like me that likes everything to be neat and tidy.

There wasn't much on the menu that I could eat because they didn't offer many options for vegetarians. I believe that I eventually settled on nachos that ended up somehow costing me around $10.

"They just spit peanut shells onto the floor?" I asked, still in shock.

There was a bucket of peanuts on our table and my friend picked up a handful. He chewed on one, using his teeth to take the peanut out of its shell, then spit the shell onto the floor.

"Yep." He said.

I didn't bother with the communal bucket of peanuts on the table because I wondered how often they refreshed them. If it was anything like the places I had worked at in the past then it wasn't very often. I have learned that while rules surrounding food safety should be of paramount importance, they are often the least regarded thing at a dining establishment.

We ate our food and were headed back home. My friend's girlfriend said that she would drive us back home because she could get us there faster. This should have been a red flag warning me to say something, but I was young and dumb and didn't say anything. I was not impressed by how the evening had gone, mostly because I was still upset by all of the spitting that went on at Logan's, so I put in my earbuds and started listening to music on my iPod Touch.

We were passing a gas station when I said, "I need to stop for coffee."

My coffee addiction at the time was at its peak and if I saw a sign for coffee, that meant I had to stop and get some. It was a crummy gas station, one that only sold a limited selection of food and watered-down coffee. I got a large coffee and a pack of powdered doughnuts. The doughnuts ended up being free because they had some kind of deal where you buy a coffee and you get a snack cake for free. I couldn't believe my luck, but little did I know, my luck was about to run out.

True to her word, my friend's girlfriend was getting us back home at record speeds. I know that this happens often with teenagers, but it is truly dumb to go over the speed limit. I try to be an extremely cautious driver, I always have, but I have so many memories of riding with teens and adults that break the speed limit on a regular basis because they are proud that they can get you somewhere faster than you normally would. I prefer to drive the speed limit, get somewhere on time, and not risk my life in the process...but that's just me.

I was listening to music on my iPod Touch and sipping

my horrible coffee when I noticed flashing lights coming from nearby. My heart lept in my chest when I realized that they were red and blue lights. The police had caught her speeding, and I was in the backseat of the car. I wondered if that made me an accomplice because I sure felt like one by not voicing my opinions on her reckless driving.

I pulled the earbuds out of my ears; everything was happening in that weird fast-slow speed that things happen in when you are experiencing something traumatic. My friend's girlfriend was freaking out in the driver's seat.

"What am I supposed to say?" She asked us.

"I don't know. You were speeding though." My friend told her.

I didn't say anything because I wondered what I would say if questioned. Is that how this would work? Would we be taken to the police station for questioning? I knew very little about our criminal justice system and it was showing.

"Ok, just everybody stay calm because I've got this." She finally said.

The police officer stood at her window as she rolled it down.

"Are you aware that you were speeding?" He asked.

She burst into tears, "Yes, but it's because my grandfather is in the hospital and I'm trying to get there to see him in time..."

I couldn't believe what I was hearing! She just lied to a police officer. What choices had I made to end up in a vehicle on the side of the interstate with someone who would lie to a police officer? The scary part is that she was so good at it. The tears came so naturally as she continued blabbering on about how sick her grandfather was.

He asked for her license and registration and then after checking a few things he told her that he would let her off with a warning, that he hoped her grandfather would be ok, and he reminded her that she still cannot go over the speed limit because if she gets pulled over again the next officer might not be so understanding. Looking back on that moment, the police officer should have followed us to the hospital and demanded to see her grandfather before letting her get away with this. Fortunately for us, he didn't because if he had then things could have been much worse than they were.

I learned to never go anywhere with that group of friends again unless I was driving, to always speak up when someone is doing something you are not comfortable with, and just avoids restaurants that allow spitting of any kind.

While it was a tough situation all around, I have not found myself in any similar situations since then. I am much choosier when it comes to picking friends, and it helps that I am almost always the one driving now. I don't intend to have any more experiences involving the police.

38

NRELUCTANT

One of the most difficult things to do when you start your journey into technology is to create a screen name that can represent you. This is something that I know a lot of people, including myself, stress over. I never considered myself an expert at naming things, though years later I would go on to make extra income as someone that names new businesses, but I have always enjoyed the challenge of finding words to represent things.

When I first got a computer the popular websites for games were Millsberry, Neopets, ToonTown, Club Penguin, and Virtual Magic Kingdom (VMK). I played Millsberry for a long time, way past the point that I realized it was just one big advertisement for General Mills and their products. It was a fun game where you could play mini-games to earn money and buy things for your character and their house.

ToonTown and Club Penguin were fun, but they were also based on business models that pretty much required you to pay to progress in the games. I needed a free option and Neopets was a perfect fit. They still have around 1.5 Million users (as of December 2020) from what I have read and this is many years after it was first released. At its height, just about everyone I knew had an account.

The thing that I liked most about Neopets was that they allowed you to create a "guild" which was essentially a webpage that you got to manage. At first, I was extremely confused because until then I had never had any experience with HTML or CSS. Online coding languages were a whole new concept for me. In order to start a guild, you needed to spend a certain amount of in-game currency to have one created. I saved my in-game money and purchased the right to own a guild.

At the time, websites offering pre-made graphics were extremely popular. MySpace helped this trend by allowing HTML and CSS codes to be copied and pasted onto their site to enhance your profile page. The websites offering pre-made graphics were seemingly endless. I learned so much about coding by having a guild page and eventually applying those same skills to edit my MySpace page. The downside of using pre-made options from other websites was that they normally would sneak some code in to advertise their website on your page. It was genius free advertising, but I wanted to learn to code so that I could create things for myself.

I eventually wanted to start my own website that would provide pre-made graphics for other sites, Neopets guilds, and MySpace pages. The crazy thing is that at the time, many of my friends were unknowingly learning HTML through copying and pasting the codes onto their pages and then sifting through them to try and remove the code for the website credits. I don't recommend ever removing credit if you use someone else's work, but that was something that was pretty common in those days.

I agonized over what a good name for my website would be. At the time websites providing graphics for guild pages were categorized as "Neo Related". I started to think of words that started with the letter "R" because I wanted to do a play on the common abbreviation "NR" for "Neo Related". After spending hours trying to think of a good name, I settled on NReluctant. The word is not grammatically correct, but it is extremely interesting to look at and has some great meaning behind it. It had the "N" in it which implied the opposite of being "reluctant". I loved it because to me it meant not being afraid to try new things and take a risk.

When people hear or see my screen name that I have kept all of these years, I almost always get asked how I came up with it. In reality, it happened just the same way that all of my stories come about. I try to think of something great and then when I stop stressing over it, the ideas happen naturally. I have stuck with that screen name all of these years because I still feel that it is representative of what I want to convey to the world. I was not afraid to try and teach myself HTML and

CSS, and while I am still not an expert at either, I am proud of the fact that it got me as far as creating my own websites and sharing that passion for learning new things with others.

39

I'M A MILLIONAIRE

One weekend, while walking through the mall, I saw a sign posted that said Books-A-Million would be coming soon. I could not believe it! The last bookstore that we had in our area was Borders and it had been closed for some time. They weren't advertising this news very much aside from the few poster sized signs around the mall, so I was hesitant to start celebrating.

About a week before they were scheduled to open, I saw some books through the window of the storefront and that is when I knew it was actually happening. We were going to have a bookstore again! I thought to myself that I would spend so much money there that they would have no choice but to stay open forever and never leave.

I immediately went home and went to the Books-A-Million website and signed up for one of their Millionaires cards. This was a discount card that would afford you 10% off of anything you bought in the store, free shipping on their website, and over $100 in coupons sent to your e-mail. The yearly cost of around $20 seemed like a bargain, especially since I knew that I would be putting that discount to good use as soon as the location at the mall opened.

I did end up spending a small fortune there as soon as they were officially opened. I spent hours browsing the books. Even though this was one of the smaller BAM locations, I took full advantage of having a selection of books to look at in-person. The experience of selecting books in-person is one that has yet to be rivaled by eBooks and digital marketplaces.

It got to a point that I was going there so often and spending so much money that I started to think about how I could spend even more time there and save even more money. I knew that I needed to get a job working there, I just wasn't sure how to make that happen since small stores like that one generally hired from a select group of applicants.

I was so excited that I made a YouTube video called "I'm A Millionaire". In the video, I talked for a few minutes about how awesome it was to be a millionaire and how I couldn't believe that it had happened to me. I even had tears in my eyes (courtesy of eye drops) to make the whole thing more believable. At the end of the video, I reveal that I got my Millionaires card from Books-A-Million and I simply couldn't believe it.

I normally Tweet a link to my YouTube videos to any companies that I talk about in the hopes that they will Tweet about my video and in return I will gain some free advertising. I wasn't expecting much when I sent my video to Books-A-Million on Twitter, but when I got a tweet back from them, I was elated. They wanted to send me a Books-A-Million gift card to say thanks for telling everyone how much I loved their store. I happily accepted the gift card, which was promptly spent upon arrival, and told them that I would love to work for them.

Again, I didn't expect much as I had never heard of anyone getting a job by Tweeting a company, but they told me to put in an application and they would reach out to the manager of the location at the mall and ask him to bring me in for an interview. I was shocked. Was this actually happening?

A few days later, I got a call from the manager at the store and he asked if I would come in for an interview. At my interview I learned a few things:

- My video had been shared around the Books-A-Million corporate offices and everyone there loved it.
- The manager at that location was a really cool person.
- They definitely wanted to hire me.

One of the questions at my interview was if I thought that I would be comfortable telling people about the Millionaires card at the checkout counter. I responded by saying that I would sure try. The manger of the store replied by saying, "Do or do not, there is no try."

I could not believe that he had just quoted Yoda from Star Wars during an interview. I definitely had to work there! I could not believe my luck, because of a YouTube video I had been hired to work at my favorite store. You have probably heard horror stories of people getting jobs at places they love to shop at and then they end up hating them, but that is not at all the case for me. I only remember my time working at Books-A-Million fondly.

I met so many fantastic individuals while working there and I was able to share my passion for books with everyone that walked through the stores entrance. My advice to anyone wanting a specific job is to do something to make yourself stand out from the competition. I live in a rural area where one might not expect there to be too many applicants at a bookstore, but it was not unusual during the time that I worked there for there to be two-hundred or more applications on file. I was determined to work there, and all that it took was me admitting to the world that I was a Millionaire.

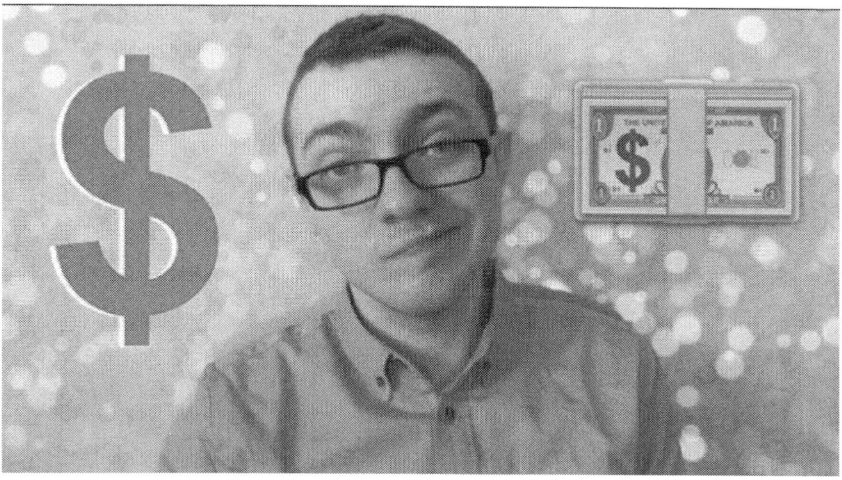

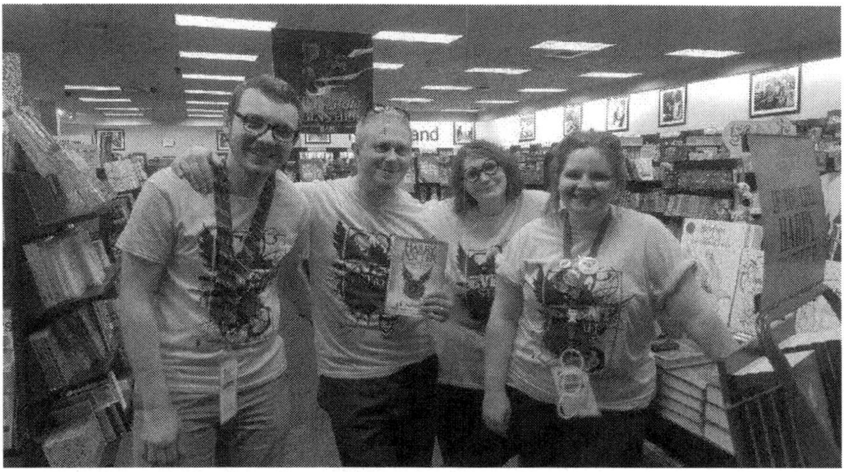

40
CONVOCATION

My first year of college, the school had a convocation for all incoming freshman. I was unsure what a convocation was, it was one of the many "college" related words that I would learn over my time spent in pursuit of a degree. It was essentially an introduction ceremony where the professors would speak and the Dean of the university would give words of encouragement to the audience.

What I found the most interesting about this event was that the professors were dressed in robes. They looked very academic, but they reminded me of the professors from Hogwarts. The campus didn't have a modern look, but it also wasn't classically old either. If the setting been a bit more medieval it would have been all the more amazing. I felt like I was getting ready to embark on an adventure that would lead to new and strange things.

When I actually started my classes, I realized that the professors each had very distinct personalities that they were not afraid to show. It was very much unlike any of the classes that I had taken in high school where the teachers had very strict guidelines on what they could say or do, and you could tell that you were never really getting to know them as a person outside of their job title. My professors were free to express themselves and this was what made those classes such a unique experience.

I would see one of my professors at the Starbucks on campus and they would genuinely ask me about how things were going. They would talk to us like we were adults, and that experience was completely new to me. Though I have had classes since then where the professor still talks down to their classes and hops in their car to drive off campus immediately after they dismiss for the day, the majority of the professors that I have had have been really interesting individuals that don't mind spending a lot of time outside of the classroom on campus.

The concept of office hours was also new to me. When class was over you could either go to a professor's office and speak to them or schedule a time to go talk to them. This made a lot of sense to me because it set clear boundaries in time when you would be able to go to a certain office and a professor would be there. Since most college campuses are quite large, if professors did not keep office hours, you would have a difficult time tracking them down.

On-campus work study jobs were almost impossible to get at the university that I attended. Once at the college I eventually transferred to, I was able to get a job. I tried to get one at the university and even did the "training" required to apply for the position, but looking back on it I see that it was a waste of time. They were hiring for a new position in one of the residence halls. The position would require you to work at the front desk.

I applied, was told to come to the training, and I got to proceed to the next step in the application process. There were about ten other guys there, and the same was supposedly going on in the girl's dorms. They said we would have to shovel snow to advance to the next part of the training. I found that alarming because I had done many job trainings and interviews in the past, but none of them ever asked me to do physical labor as part of the application process.

It was freezing cold outside, but the group of applicants, including myself, shoveled the walkways clear. It took about an hour and a half and by the end I was truly asking myself if the job would be worth all of this.

"Congrats! You all get to move on to the next part of the application!" One of the employees at the residence hall told us.

As I trudged back to my dorm in one of the older buildings, I got the sinking feeling that we had just worked for free for a position that only one person would get. If I didn't get the position, then that was equivalent to a wasted hour and a half of work. I couldn't help but think about things in these terms because I was paying for my education out-of-pocket and the few student loans that I did have I was attempting to pay off as quickly as I borrowed them. I have never been able to be comfortable with the idea of having debt, so I find that I tend to pay loans off in advance.

The next part of the application process was to be held at a newly constructed chapel and event space on campus. It was the nicest building on campus and therefore it tended to be booked-out well in advance for weddings and corporate events. I was just excited that we would be indoors for this part of the process. When I walked in, there were twice as many girls as there were guys. The position at the girl's dorm had twice the people competing for it. I felt a little better about my odds when I saw this.

They had us do terrible team building exercises for hours. It didn't make much sense because there were only two total positions for this group of thirty individuals that didn't know each other and would probably never speak again after the positions had been filled. There were no winners, only those of us who attended and therefore qualified to go on to the final round. The interview was to be the last step before they would decide who to hire.

The whole process up to that point had been humiliating and ridiculous. The job only paid minimum wage, but for the chance to sit at a desk and do homework while getting paid it seemed worth it at the time. I went to the interview a few days later, waited about an hour for them to call my name, and then realized that one of the three guys interviewing me was the brother of one of the other applicants.

I decided not to let that fact get to me. They asked a series of questions that were completely unrelated to how qualified you would actually be to manage a front desk a few hours each evening. Instead of asking questions that would determine how reliable we would be, they asked things like, "If you were shrunk down to where you could fit into a blender, and someone stuck you in that blender, how would you get out?"

I was caught off-guard by the questions, but I think I answered them pretty well.

"I would stand atop one of the blades, jump when the blender gets turned on, and let the force propel me out the top." I said, feeling pretty confident that my answer made as much sense as anyone could hope for when asked a random question like that.

They nodded looking quizzically and said, "Ok, I suppose that is a good idea."

I could tell that I had very little in common with the members of staff that were interviewing me for the position. I mean, one guy shared some of the same DNA as one of the interviewers and I couldn't even impress them with an answer to a question. When it was all over, I went back to my dorm, not able to get the newfound information about the interviewer and his brother out of my head.

A few days later when they announced who got the job, it came as no surprise to anyone that the interviewer's brother was who they hired. I knew the guy because he was dating one of my friends from class, he was a nice person but not nearly as qualified for the position as some of the others, myself included. This seems to be common at almost all of the workplaces I have been a part of, save a few good ones that only hire based on credentials and qualifications.

There were many small lessons that I would learn from my time in college, not all academic related. I learned that there are students that make a schedule of their favorite television shows and take that with them to their advisor's office when scheduling their classes. I knew someone that did this; she would not miss the show Glee for anything, especially not anything as inconsequential as a class. These students would risk having to attend college another semester to a year if it meant not missing a show they liked.

I also learned that some people take their group identities very seriously. I had some friends who were huge fans of Harry Potter. They made it very clear to me that they were members of the house Hufflepuff. They had another friend who got sorted into Slytherin. The one who got sorted into Slytherin lived in the same building that I did. I saw him sitting in the common room crying and asked him what was wrong.

"I don't know what to do." He said desperately.

I was sure that he had just gotten some terrible life-altering news.

"What happened?"

Between tears and gasps for breath he said, "I got sorted into Slytherin."

I looked around the room to see if anyone else were there to hear this, they weren't. Normally there was a group of students playing Magic cards and they rarely left. I never saw any of them in class and more often than not, they were in the common room playing cards. I think they paid tuition and room-and-board just for the privilege to sit there and play games.

"So, it's not a big deal. Just take the test again." I said trying to reason with him.

"I did. It's the same every time. I wanted to be in Hufflepuff so badly..." He continued to cry.

I knew as well as he did that our other friends who were Hufflepuff and took it seriously would likely disown him after they found out. I wasn't sure how to help him because I never imagined that I would be a part of a situation like this.

He got out his cellphone and called someone, "Mom...I have some bad news."

He was still crying, "I got sorted into Slytherin and there's nothing that I can do about it."

I imagined that his mother would probably be able to console him in some way.

"I did! I took it multiple times and it's the same every time." He shouted into the phone.

Nothing that anyone could say would make him feel any better about this. I had taken the test on Pottermore when it was released and was sorted into Ravenclaw, but I didn't take it seriously because at the end of the day it isn't real. When our other friends found out that he had been sorted into Slytherin, they definitely treated him differently. They agreed that since he was a Slytherin who wanted to be a Hufflepuff he could continue to be their friend, but he was always on the outside of their group after that.

Hoping that it would diffuse some of the tension, I told them that I was a Ravenclaw. They weren't as alarmed by this because Ravenclaw is known for being studious and Luna Lovegood was in that house so we couldn't be all that bad. They treated me differently after that too. It was strange because Hufflepuff isn't known for being mean or exhibiting traits of a stereotypical clique. They actually acted more like Slytherins than true Hufflepuffs, but I wasn't going to be the one to bring that up.

I recall one lunch in particular where it became clear that I needed to call it quits on our friendship.

"My uncle draws comics and is going to be at the convention next week." One of them said.

She was talking about an anime convention that was happening about three hours away. It was a popular out-of-town event that a lot of students at my university attended.

"That's cool, but not professionally right?" I asked, genuinely curious.

She looked at the others at the table and then to me, "Are you serious? That's such a Ravenclaw thing to say."

The others nodded in agreement.

"I was just wondering because there usually aren't a lot of

professional artist there, just hobbyist and independent artist." I said.

"Ravenclaw's are so rude." One of the others said.

"Yeah, I'm done eating." Said the third.

They got up and left the dining hall. I wondered what had just happened? It seemed like something you would see in a movie. I didn't think that people took these things so seriously, but what I learned in college is that some people have hobbies and interests while others have obsessions that start to define them. I don't think it is healthy to adopt a fictional world as your reality. I love fiction, but you have to be able to tell the two apart.

I got a Facebook message shortly after that, where the one who said her uncle drew comics told me, "I did like you. Like, I really liked you, but I just don't think it would ever work between us."

She didn't have to say it explicitly in words, but I knew that she would never date anyone outside of the Hufflepuff house. Honestly, with that kind of obsessive disconnect from reality she probably won't ever date anyone at all. I wish all of them the best and hope that they are happy in whatever world they are currently living.

I learned a lot from my classes at college, but I think I learned more about people and their behaviors more than anything else. A high school setting is limited to specific behaviors that rarely deviate from expected norms. A college setting allows for whatever type of expression you deem normal. There are rules, but no restrictions on personality and letting that effect how you procure your education. I never would have expected the crazy things that happened, to have actually happened, as I sat there as a freshman at the convocation watching my future professors sit on stage while wearing their robes.

41

HAUNTED HALLS

The dormitory that I lived in at the university that I attended was famous for being haunted. There were some amazing new dorms that had been built a few years previous, but those cost more due to the fact that they were newer and had decent heating and cooling in the rooms. The building where I lived was the oldest dorm on campus and it truly showed.

The parquet floor tiles were coming up throughout most of my room and there were many spots where there was just leftover residue from whatever binding chemical had been used to make the wood stick all those many years ago when the building was built. There was a singular sink in each room, crazy hot radiator heating, and no cooling when the temperature got too high. The worst part is how much it cost me to live in that building.

While I did not finish my education at that university, I was there long enough to experience some pretty strange things. There was one other dorm building that was known to be haunted and it just so happened that it was the girl's dorm that was only a few feet from the building I was in. Who knows why those two buildings were known for being haunted, I cannot say for sure, but I can tell you what I experienced while living there.

The third floor of the residence hall that I lived in was reserved for females only. The story was that years ago there was a depressed student living in that building. She painted a picture of Marilyn Monroe on the wall of her room and then killed herself. Now, I do not take the topic of suicide lightly, and I truly hope that this was only a ghost story told to frighten those who lived on campus, but it was a story that I was told many times over the course of my time spent at that school.

It was also said that over the years they had tried to paint over the wall many times, but that the painting done by that particular student kept bleeding through. Since I was a male and didn't know anyone that lived on the third floor of my building, I had no way to verify the information. I did have friends who lived in the residence hall next door, in the other supposedly haunted building.

One of my friends who lived there came to class one day and she looked terrified. She was on the verge of crying so I knew that something had to be wrong.

"Are you okay?" I asked her.

"No." She said.

"What's wrong?"

She looked at me seriously and said, "I think I just saw a ghost."

She told me that every morning she would use the floor length hall mirror that was set up on her floor of the residence hall to check and see how her outfit looked. This was actually a pretty common feature of those residence halls as I had been told by others who lived there that the residents frequently checked their outfits in those mirrors. She saw a girl standing behind her when she looked into the mirror, and it startled her so she turned around.

When she turned around, there was no one there. She looked back to the mirror and only saw herself. After searching the hallway, she determined that she was the only person there at that time.

"It was a ghost. It had to be. People had told me about her, but I didn't believe them until today." She said, her voice shaking.

I didn't think too much of this at the time because while I did believe that she was genuinely frightened by something, I wasn't sure that she had seen a ghost. Perhaps she had merely seen her reflection refract strangely against the light. Every so often I would hear a similar story coming from one of the residents in that building. Up to that point, the residence halls where I lived were pretty normal, aside from my roommate.

My first experience that was not normal was on a random

weekday morning. I was getting ready to leave the building when I heard a voice coming from the stairwell. As I got closer, I could tell that it was the sound of someone singing. I opened the door to the stairs and heard an amazing voice singing calm Celtic songs that echoed perfectly in the stairwell. I couldn't see anyone, but there was definitely someone there singing. I had never imaged that someone would be confident enough, or comfortable enough living in a dorm, that they would treat it like their home and sing in public. I didn't want to be late for class, so I left wondering who was singing, hoping that I would hear them again sometime.

A few days passed and I didn't hear any singing. I made it a point to listen by the stairwell each morning on my way to class to try and hear something...anything. When I thought that perhaps I had imagined hearing the songs, I heard it again. There was definitely someone singing in the stairwell. This time I decided to find out who it was, and at the very least compliment them on their talent.

I walked up the steps to the first landing and still didn't see anyone. When I made it to the second landing, I saw a girl, about my age, sitting on the steps and singing as if nobody else was around. Her voice was peaceful, and it did not surprise me to learn that she was studying Music at the university. I complimented her on her singing, and I have to admit that I was more than a little relieved that it was an actual human singing and not an apparition.

The next strange thing that happened to me occurred at night. The hallways were a bit creepy at night because they were generally empty and only slightly well-lit. The bathroom and showers were communal and therefore I had to leave my room to walk down the hall and take a shower. The shower stalls were some of the strangest that I have ever seen. They were circular, like a pod, and they didn't have doors on them, but when you walked into one there was an arch that shielded you from view. The best way that I can explain it is like a conch shell, you can clearly see that there is an opening, but whatever lies beyond that opening is hidden.

Nothing strange had ever happened before while I showered, and for the most part I was the only one ever there. Either everyone else on my floor showered exclusively in the mornings or didn't bother with it at all. I wasn't complaining; it was nice to never have a line to wait in to use the bathroom. I was showering when I heard a sound like someone saying something. I couldn't make out what they were saying, so I turned the water pressure down and listened more carefully.

"James." The voice said.

It sounded like a young female was talking and they had just said my name. This was one of the male-only floors of the residence hall, and it being late at night there should have been no one allowed on the floor that didn't live there. I turned off the shower and looked around, but I didn't see anyone. I walked over to the window that was propped open and served as the only ventilation in the small room, but I didn't see anyone outside either. I had thought that maybe someone's voice had carried its way up and through the window, but that was not the case.

The door to the bathroom was loud and would screech when opened, and since I hadn't heard the door open, I knew that nobody had actually entered the room. I went back and finished my shower, deciding that it was only my imagination. All of the ghost tales and stories of what my friends had experienced on campus were starting to get to me. When I was finished showering, I went over to the window that I always closed in case the weather got bad overnight so that rain or snow would not blow in, and sitting on the window sill was a small silver bracelet that had not been there before.

I looked around, and yet again, there was no one else there but myself. I had not imagined everything, and the bracelet was proof of that. I contemplated taking the bracelet with me so that I would have some evidence, if only for myself, that what I thought had happened had actually occurred, but I left it sitting on the windowsill. The silver shone in contrast to the chipped white paint that had covered the sill for many years.

The next day, I went back to see if the bracelet was still there. It was gone. I will never know if someone else took it or if whatever left it there in the first place had come back to reclaim it. After that, I took any stories of my friends' experiences seriously. There were many instances where the window in the bathroom would sound as if it had slammed shut but when I would check it would still be open. I don't know how many of the stories on campus were true, but what I do know is that something strange is definitely going on there. Since I lived there, that residence hall has been shut down. I have been told it was due to the age of the building, but my personal guess is that it has something to do with all of the hauntings.

42

VOLUNTEER

While in college I was part of a volunteer program. The program would award students with a stipend to help cover the cost of tuition once each semester in exchange for around 170 hours of volunteer work and attendance to trainings. I met a lot of friends in this program as I tended to spend most of my time with them working on volunteer projects.

My regular location for volunteering was The Room Upstairs as they were a non-profit art program during the day. When I wasn't working there, I was doing volunteer opportunities offered by the program. These were things like helping clean a local national park. The work was often more difficult than having a paying job, but it was a great experience, and I got a lot more out of it than tuition money.

The program announced that there would be an opportunity to volunteer in Asheville, North Carolina for a week over spring break. Spots on this trip were limited and details about what we would be doing were vague. I logged on immediately at the given time and registered to secure my spot on this trip. Not only would I earn a ton of volunteer hours that I needed, but I had been the The Biltmore Estate many times before and already knew that I liked Asheville.

When we arrived in Asheville we were greeted by a rundown motel. I didn't know most of the people on that trip who were with me because that opportunity was also given to students at the university's other campus. I went into my room with my roommate, a complete stranger by all accounts, and was shocked at the condition of things. There was very little lighting and the room felt more like a cave than some place to stay.

I pulled back the sheets on the bed, something I do immediately upon entering any hotel room, to check and see if they had been cleaned. There were long hairs clinging to the cream-colored sheets. I told my roommate and he said, "I don't care, it doesn't bother me. It's just some hair."

He walked over to my bed to examine what I was complaining about and started picking a few of the hairs off of the sheets. I left the room and went directly to the front desk.

"There is hair all over my bed. I don't think my room was cleaned before I got here." I said.

The person working at the desk sighed and said, "I'm not sure what you want me to do."

I could not believe it, there was no way I would be staying in that room or sleeping in that bed.

"Can you have someone clean the room?" I asked.

"I can just put you in a different room if that would make you happy." They replied.

I went back to the room and told my roommate that we were moving to a room down the hall. He seemed annoyed that he had to move his single duffel bag from our current room to another, but I didn't care because I was not sleeping in that bed. The other room was not much better, but at least the sheets didn't have hair stuck to them. I cannot confidently say that the room was "clean", but I knew that complaining to the desk clerk would get me nowhere.

Our first volunteer assignment was to work at a community garden. On the surface this doesn't sound like it would be too difficult, but we were setting up a garden from scratch. The organization we worked with had waited for us to arrive to get started on the wooden structures that much of the fruits and vegetables would be grown in.

We spent most of that evening clearing the ground and getting it ready for the materials to be put together. Each day we would be working with a different non-profit, so at least I had the assurance that whatever we did next might not be as difficult. At the end of that day, I was happy knowing that we had played a small part in preparing the community garden that would help to feed local families.

When we arrived back to the motel, I stared into the empty pool that was the centerpiece. I was exhausted and just wanted to take a shower and get some sleep. The next day we worked with an organization that helped homeless individuals get their first place to live. This was an extremely impactful experience for me.

We worked loading and unloading a moving truck full of donated furniture. We drove for about thirty minutes until we arrived at an apartment complex. It took us about an hour to move all of the furniture into one of the empty apartments. It was a simple place, a one-bedroom apartment, but when I saw the reaction on the man's face who would be living there, I understood that it was so much more than that.

The man moving into his first apartment had been abandoned by his parents as a teenager to live on the streets because he had mental and physical disabilities. The non-profit explained to us that they had been helping him get a bank account set up, learn how to use public transit, and ride the bus from the apartment complex to their offices downtown. He would not be able to work because of his physical disabilities, but he was expected to check-in at their offices a few times each week.

You would have thought by the smile on his face that we had just moved him into a mansion. I could not believe that anyone would throw their child out onto the streets, let alone someone that was as defenseless as this man was. I am grateful for non-profits like this one because many years ago when I visited Atlanta and saw the homeless individuals living there, I started to wonder if anyone cared enough to help. I was getting to be one of the ones helping them, and that is something that money cannot buy.

There were little moments throughout the week when we were given free time to shop and eat downtown. I had also scheduled with our group leader some time to visit The Biltmore Estate with those in our group who had never been before and wanted to see it.

When we visited The Biltmore Estate only a few others wanted to go. The rest went to ride Segways around the downtown area. There were only about five of us in my group, but I enjoyed that time just as much as I have ever enjoyed touring the estate. Two of the others with me were mainly focused on getting a few bottles of wine to take back to their motel room. We were not supposed to have alcohol on the trip because it was a school trip. This was not an issue for me because I do not drink alcohol, but those two women were determined to buy some.

I should have known that they planned on getting wine from the start when they showed up with massive purses that day the size of tote bags. I toured the estate with one of my friends that had come along, and the two women went off in search of wine.

Those two were especially giggly on the ride back to the motel, so I assume they had tasted some of the product that was clinking up against one another in their purses.

"I have a tattoo." One of them said.

Nobody knew where that had come from, but one of the others in the group said, "Oh cool, let us see it."

She giggled and raised her pants leg to reveal a blurry drawing of what looked like a rat with wings.

"It isn't very good because my friend did it when they were…drunk." She said, her words slurring.

We all agreed that it truly looked like a large rat with wings. Anyone would be hard pressed to disagree, especially given the fact that the "fairy" had a long tail that curled around like one on a rodent. I felt bad for her because while she thought that she had this amazing story to tell about how she got her drunken rat fairy tattoo, all I was hearing was someone that was missing something somewhere in her life. I couldn't fathom why anyone would be proud of something like that.

When we arrived back at the motel, things got weirder. The two women knocked on my room door and when I opened it, they were having a hard time standing up. It is a wonder that our group leader did not see them and send them home immediately.

"We are about to open a new bottle in our room if you guys want to come over. We are inviting everyone!" They said, laughing as if they had just told a funny joke.

"No thanks. I'm tired and want to catch up on some rest." I said.

They didn't seem disappointed because in their minds this trip was just one big party and if I didn't want to be a part of it then they would surely find someone else who would. My roommate was also not interested, as nobody wanted to get kicked off of a volunteer trip. I mean it just sounds ridiculous when you think of getting booted off of a trip meant to help others.

They left and I shut and locked the door. This motel was sketchy to say the least. Though I have stayed in some pretty rundown places, like the "resort" where I had to prop my door shut with a chair because the door wouldn't close properly, this was probably the worst.

I heard a sound coming from somewhere outside my locked door. It was getting louder. I opened my door to try and hear what was going on.

"Help! Help!" Someone screamed from one of the rooms across the hall.

I immediately called the front desk because the screaming did not stop, it only kept getting louder and more desperate.

"Yes, we're aware of the situation. The police have been informed." They said in the same nonchalant tone that they used when I complained to them about my room earlier in the week.

I shut my door and kept it locked. About ten minutes later I heard the police shouting from the hallway for the person to open their door. This went on for about ten more minutes until the police got into the room, presumably with a spare key from the front desk, and the shouting got even louder. I cracked open my door enough to be able to better hear what was going on, and from what I gathered, there was a husband and wife in that room having a fight that got out of hand. They took the husband away in handcuffs.

The rest of the night was uneventful, thankfully. The next day we volunteered at a soup kitchen. This was the day that I learned about the businesses that donate food at the end of each day. Panera Bread was one of those businesses. There was so much Panera Bread that we were able to hand out everything from cookies to loaves of bread to everyone waiting in line for their meal. We served them a meal consisting of salad and a burger, and then they got to choose a few items from Panera Bread to take with them.

There was an older lady overseeing the soup kitchen. She had blond hair that was blown-out and extremely long fingernails that had been painted bright colors. The fingernails were so long that they were curving at the ends, and I wondered how she was able to pick things up with them. This was not a difficult job, but it was definitely rewarding getting to give the gift of food to those in need.

I did not realize how many people are homeless, even in a city as small as Asheville, North Carolina, until this trip. It was an eye-opening experience to say the least. After we left there we went to an older looking motel and I was a bit confused about why we were there until we went inside. This motel had been purchased by a non-profit and was repurposed to provide housing to homeless veterans. Now, I do not believe that anyone should have to experience homelessness, but especially not veterans.

There were hundreds of veterans, people who had fought for my freedoms as an American citizen, waiting on a list to get temporary housing at this motel. If you have ever been to a motel before you know that the rooms are not extremely large. There were anywhere from four to six veterans housed in each of those rooms and there still were not enough rooms to accommodate all of them.

Thankfully, there were common areas where they could spend time outside of their rooms if they needed some more personal space. There was a large cafeteria that served three basic meals per day, an area with tables and chairs for them to sit and talk to one another, and a few outdoor areas with benches. It wasn't anything fancy, but it was serving a purpose in a community that desperately needed it.

Our job was to clean some of the rooms so that they could be ready for new residents. The hotel was fighting the battle of getting the rooms habitable because this was a fairly recent project. The quicker the rooms were cleaned and prepared, the quicker they could move more veterans in. The rooms that I worked on were in terrible condition. They appeared as if they had never been cleaned and had been left sitting for many years after the place originally shut down.

After I helped clean a few of the rooms, I worked on washing the windows outside. This was an older motel with a classic look to it. The exteriors of the rooms were covered in large panes of glass, though they hadn't been cleaned in ages and anyone driving past on the road might think they were not windows at all, but rather gray-brown walls.

That was a long day of cleaning, but my Papaw is a Vietnam War veteran and that was all that I could think about when working there. It could just as easily have been him in need of a place to live. What I have learned from working with the homeless population is that we are all one big hospital bill or tragedy away from being homeless. Very few people have a safety-net big enough to account for some of the tragedies of life. I also learned that aside from lacking money, most all of these people had been lacking a moral support system.

When you don't have anyone there to pick you up when you fall down, often times you just stay down. I was thankful that non-profits and organizations were trying to be that support system. It was sad to see that things had to get extremely bad for someone to step in and help, but it was also encouraging that people were trying to make things better.

It was about time for us to leave for the day. We were waiting in the hallway as our group took turns using the bathroom.

"You can't be serious. You eat dog in your country?" Someone in our group was asking one of the foreign students that had joined us on the trip.

The student was from Vietnam and before I even looked, I knew who was asking the question. Miss Rat Fairy was in shock when the student from Vietnam replied, "Yes."

He explained to her that he didn't see it as being any different than how we eat cows and pigs in America. I understood his perspective and explanation that it was only a matter of social norms, but she was not having any of it.

"I'm sorry, but that's just disgusting." She said.

I didn't want to be a part of that conversation, so I tuned out the rest of what was said. I assume it was more of them arguing over if it was ethical to eat a dog. I had been a vegetarian for a while, so they honestly didn't want me giving my opinion on eating any kind of meat.

The trip was set to end with a big dinner at a place that had a unique premise. It was an old church that hosted community dinners where everyone was welcome. The homeless population would help cook the meals alongside everyone else and then the community would all sit together at large tables and have a meal. The idea was to forget everything about socioeconomic status and people's differences to come together and celebrate humanity with a meal. It was such a cool place!

The food being cooked was mostly meat-based, so I wouldn't be eating a lot of it, but I still loved the idea. I got my plate and unfortunately did not eat much because when I looked down there was a very large hair stuck to it. I didn't want to be too picky considering the purpose of the event, and I was sitting at a table with some truly inspiring individuals, so I didn't mention the hair, but I wasn't able to eat much either. There was so much food being passed around and I had already stated that I was a vegetarian, so thankfully nobody seemed to notice.

I loved being a part of these amazing events. The week had seemed to fly by, and I hope that we were able to make a lasting impact, even if it was in some small way. Seeing the local community in Asheville come together to try and make a change was something that I will never forget. While the motel accommodations were less than desirable and some of the members of my group didn't mesh well with others, I still came away from the experience with some new friends and memories that I will cherish forever.

43

ROOMMATE

You've probably already guessed that I don't do well with roommates. I am the type of person that likes things to be a specific way, and I am also someone that has to have alone time. Don't get me wrong, I love spending time with my friends and family, but if I am with someone for more than six hours then I really have to like you. I am also a fairly private person, which makes this book one of the most difficult that I have ever written. That being said, to have to share my personal space with someone has never worked well for me.

No matter how much I really do like the person, I start to become irritated by the smallest things when I am with them for extended periods of time. Apply all of this information about me to the situation of having a roommate. I genuinely enjoy being around friends and family and have no problem going on extended trips with them either, but in terms of my living space, I have to have it all to myself. That probably sounds a bit selfish, but I tell you this because it is for everyone's benefit. I am not a fun person to be around when I am annoyed and stressed over having to share my space with someone else.

I never really did sleepovers and things like that when I was a kid because I didn't like the idea of having to live at someone else's house, if only for a night. Maybe it is because I never learned how to make myself at home in a stranger's house that I don't do well with roommates, or maybe I would have always been like this regardless of how many sleepovers I had.

I lived on campus my first semester of college. The cost of having a single room, without a roommate, was even more ridiculous than the cost of having a double. I signed up to have a roommate, filled out a survey that was supposed to match me perfectly with someone that I would have things in common with, and took out student loans to cover the cost. The day arrived for me to move into my dorm and my parents, brother, and Nanny and Papaw were there to help. My roommate did not arrive until after my family had left so they never really had the pleasure of meeting him.

I was moving things around and placing them where I wanted, when I heard someone coming towards the room. A moment later the person I presumed to be my roommate entered with his parents. He sat his few belongings on his bed and looked around the room. His parents did not seem very happy about something, either their son having to live in a tiny room with a stranger or him going to college in general.

"Hi, it's nice to meet you." I said.

His mother looked at me and then to my Keurig Mini and then back to me, "You're not allowed to have that."

I was taken aback...were her first words to me really going to be something about not being able to have a Keurig? As an avid coffee drinker, I had read the rule book thoroughly on the topic of having a coffee maker in my dorm room and Keurig coffee makers were absolutely allowed because they did not have any exposed heating elements.

"Oh, no, it's not a problem. I read the rules and these ARE allowed." I said, trying to smile as best as I could.

She raised an eyebrow and then looked to her husband, "We'll talk to the R.A. about it before we leave."

There are many abbreviations like "R.A." that you learn when you first arrive to college, by "R.A." she meant our resident advisor. That would have been the person responsible for making sure everyone follows the rules in the residence hall. I hoped that she would go talk to the R.A. about it because they would surely tell her that she was mistaken.

They looked to their son and said, "Let's go eat."

He got up without saying a word, something that would be his trademark over the time that I lived there, and left with them. Later that evening he returned but they were not with him. It was perhaps one of the worst introductions I have ever had and to this day I still don't know what their problem was.

I don't know who matched us as roommates or if they even put any effort into it, but the next few months were not enjoyable. You probably won't believe me when I tell you that he never really spoke to me, but it is true. As far as dorm rooms go, ours probably broke records for being one of the quietest. I made attempts to talk to him, but it just got weird after a while when he clearly didn't want to have conversations.

One night, I heard a sound, so I awoke to see him sitting up in his bed and staring at the wall. I was not sure what was going on, but it freaked me out. Here I was living with a stranger and they were just staring at the wall for extended periods of time in the middle of the night. This ended up being a frequent occurrence.

I gathered that he was also a very shy person, something I can actually relate to. There was a sink in our room but no bathroom, it was pretty useless except for brushing teeth. He never would brush his teeth when I was around and more than once he actually took his toothbrush and toothpaste down the hall to the public bathroom. We had tiny closets with wooden doors, and he would go inside of his closet to change clothes.

I just started to feel very weird living there, like somehow, I was an intruder in that room. I was disappointed that for what I was paying to live there I was having such a terrible experience. All that I wanted was just a normal roommate that I could talk to occasionally and a quiet room to study in...well, I got the quiet room.

I let a lot of this go and tried not to focus on it because I assumed that it was his personality and that perhaps he was just a very introverted person. Until one day, a group of my friends from the volunteer program I was a part of, started talking about how great my roommate was.

"You got lucky, he's such a nice guy." One of the girls in the group said.

I could tell by the way that she was talking about him that she had a crush. My suspicions were later confirmed when they started dating.

"Yeah, he is so great." Another said.

Surely, they had to be joking with me.

"Are you serious?" I said.

They looked confused, almost as confused as I was.

"Yeah. What? You don't think he's nice?"

"Umm, we have literally never had a conversation."

They didn't believe me at first, but after weeks of hearing these same complaints they finally determined that maybe he just didn't like me. I could have guessed as much myself. I decided that I would make myself as much at home as I could while I was there because I was spending a small fortune to stay on campus.

I didn't watch my television very much, but I did watch the new episodes of my favorite show, The Office, when they would air. I knew some people who would schedule their classes around their T.V. schedule, there were a shocking number of students who did this, but I was happy just to watch an episode on the occasion.

My roommate loved his television. After a month or so of living there, it got to the point that from the time he would come in the room he would turn it on and leave it on until after I turned the lights off and went to bed. I was always the one who had to turn the lights off because I believe he would have stayed up round the clock watching that T.V. I would wait until around 2 A.M., and having a class in a few hours I would walk to his side of the room where the light switch was located and flip it off. I had hoped that he would eventually take the cue to turn it off himself, but he never did.

America's Next Top Model seemed to be a favorite of his and he would turn the volume up quite loudly. Midterms were approaching and we were all asked to be quiet in the evenings. He seemed to take this more as a suggestion rather than a rule, so life in our dorm room went on awkwardly as it always had. I was getting frustrated trying to focus on my studies between shouts from Heidi Klum about how great a dress looked, so I decided to take matters into my own hands.

It was not uncommon for the RA at our residence hall to slide notices under our door to let us know about upcoming events or new rules to follow. I decided that I would make a notice of my own. My roommate never picked them up off of the floor, rather he would leave them until I got there to clean up, so I knew that he would not pick mine up to inspect it, but I also knew that he had to be reading them because if they mentioned quiet hours, the television on his side of the room would tend to be a bit less loud.

I stated on the paper that there needed to be absolute quiet after 5 P.M. I figured that was reasonable enough, especially during midterms. I went outside of the room and slid the paper underneath the door, just as the RA normally does, then I left to get some lunch and waited to see what would happen. For the first evening or two it worked, he didn't watch television at all, but on the third day, he had a marathon of America's Next Top Model and blasted the volume.

One evening I checked his Facebook to see where he had gone. It had been three days since he was in the dorm room and I wondered if he had decided to stay off campus. I discovered that his aunt had passed away. When he finally arrived back, I told him that I saw online that his aunt had passed away and that I was sorry to hear about it. I had lost my aunt a few years back and it was a very difficult thing to go through.

He nodded and said, "Thanks."

It was the closest to having a conversation that we ever got. I tend to overthink everything and one part of that is trying to see every situation from different perspectives. I tried to understand why he acted the way that he did and why he didn't want to get to know me.

A few weeks passed and he disappeared again. I looked online to see what was going on and discovered that he was going somewhere to stand in a creek. It was a strange statement for someone to make, but in this situation, it actually didn't seem that weird. About a week later he came back and from what I heard from my friends that liked him, he indeed went somewhere to stand in a creek.

When it came down to the facts, it might have been that he didn't really want a roommate any more than I did. I wish that I had known that to be the case because that was one thing that we could have had in common and discussed. I told the RA that I would need a single room, or I would be leaving the university. The RA said they would get me a single room immediately, but of course they never did. Since I couldn't justify paying a large sum of money to live in an uncomfortable situation, I left that school and enrolled at another where I was able to commute and live at home.

Perhaps his plan from the start was to make things so awkward that I would leave. If that was the case, then I think his plan backfired because I am positive that the university would have placed someone else in that room with him. There was no way they were going to let potential room and board money slip through the cracks. I doubt that he would have liked having a roommate that was loud, messy, and disrespectful, but the odds were pretty good that is exactly what he ended up getting.

In the end I learned that I do not like having a roommate. It is essential that I have my alone time. I truly like having time to think and do whatever I want. There are people that I love having in my life, but I would be lying if I said that I don't appreciate the moments that I have by myself too. I know that my roommate that semester could have been much worse, but my expectations were not extremely high to begin with. For what schools charge to live on campus, more consideration should be taken when pairing people as roommates.

44

LIBRARY OF SECRETS

There were few places on campus where I could get peace and quiet if I wanted to read. I quickly discovered where those places were. There were student seating areas in some of the buildings, one in the student center that I would use between classes, as well as a few buildings that seemed to only have a class or two in them, so they were mostly empty.

The library was an obvious choice and it just so happened that the university that I attended had an award-winning library that had been nationally recognized. Inside of the library you could always find students typing away at the public computers, occasionally paying to print a few pages of their assignment. They had an excellent selection of curated books as well as an impressive collection of movies that you could check out. I love to read, but I think I used the library more for checking-out movies to watch on my laptop than for getting books. Until then, I was unaware that libraries normally have collections of movies that you can borrow.

The library had two floors that I knew of and was connected to one of the other buildings that housed a lot of my classes. One evening I decided to explore some of the different sections of the building that I had never been to. The layout of the building was very interesting to me as there were stairs leading to various sections that I would discover by accident. It was on this evening that I saw a student seemingly disappear. One moment they were browsing a bookshelf and the next they were...gone.

I went to where the student had been standing and searched for where they could possibly have gone. I heard them nearby and then discovered that hidden amongst the shelves, there was an opening just big enough for a person to walk through that led to a different section of the library. I had walked past that bookshelf many times and never thought that there was anything behind it. The way that the shelf was positioned made it appear as if there was a wall behind it, when in reality an entire section of the library was there.

I was excited to find that this area of the library existed. I started taking my books and assignments there whenever I had time between classes. I showed the "secret" area of the library to a few friends who were also shocked to find that it existed. There were a few tables in the back of this section and a few old chairs. It seemed that nobody really knew about this quiet spot as I was almost always the only person there.

One day I was surprised when I went to that part of the library and a woman was sitting at the table reading.

"Oh, hello." She said.

She seemed slightly annoyed and a bit surprised to see me.

"Hello." I said.

"I come here because it's quiet." She said, clearly wondering if I was there to disturb her peace.

"Me too. Nobody seems to know about it." I replied.

Her expression lightened and we started talking about some of the classes that we both enjoyed. We both agreed that this part of the library was best kept a secret, otherwise it wouldn't be special anymore. I never saw her again after that, but I assume she was still coming back because I would occasionally find forgotten papers on the table with her name on them.

It occurred to me to look at some of the books in this section of the building. They were strange titles, many of which made little-to-no sense. They covered odd topics, many about mysteries and things that might otherwise be categorized as fiction but were labeled as non-fiction there. This secret part of the library contained books that didn't seem to belong anywhere else.

That was always my go-to spot for studying after I discovered it. I just as easily could have never known that it was there, had I not seen a student disappear into the stacks that day. It makes me wonder how many places I have missed seeing because I simply didn't know that they exist. I wonder about this in relation to my hometown. We live somewhere our whole lives and only ever see a small part of it. We know that there must be more, places that have been undiscovered or unseen by our eyes, but we rarely ever question these things.

I don't think that I ever uncovered all of the mysteries of that library, and some part of me likes it that way. I hope that someone else has started going there since I left the school, someone that will appreciate the peace and quiet. Perhaps they will even read some of the obscure tomes that line the shelves, or maybe they will tell everyone they know about the room and ruin the mystery of the place. It is just something that I will never know, one more mystery about my library of secrets.

45

DON'T PANIC

There are times in life when we all get overwhelmed. In a world where we have expectations coming from everyone we know and even those we don't, standards that are impossible to live up to, and a constant bombardment of information, it is hard not to feel stressed.

When I was in college, I needed to take a Physical Science class in order to progress in my program of study. The professor for that class was new to the school and seemed nice. She was extremely experienced having previously worked as a physicist. She was nice on the first day of class but told us that she had a temper and there would be days that we wouldn't really want to be around her. I should have taken that as my first warning sign that something wasn't right, but I assumed that she was just trying to be relatable and show some personality.

Along with everyone else in the class, I quickly realized that she was not teaching the class in a manner that we would be able to understand. She was teaching as if we were Science majors and planning to have a career directly involving Physics. I may be mistaken, but Physics and Physical Science are two different classes, right? I looked it up online and am more confused now than I was before, apparently Physics is a Physical Science, but Physical Science can involve other "physical" Sciences.

We were all Education majors, so being taught as if we were Science majors was overwhelming. After the first two weeks, over half of the class had dropped from the course and opted to pay extra to take it online over the summer at a nearby community and technical college. The credit would transfer from the online class, so almost everyone saw it as the more logical option. I decided to stick around a bit longer and suffer in the hopes that it would get better.

It didn't. Seeing that more than half of her students had dropped the class, she increased the difficulty level and offered to stay late to help us after-hours if we needed it. Obviously, we needed the help, but looking back on the situation there was no way I was ever going to do well in her class. I hadn't had the necessary Math classes to do well on the Math portions, I was only ever required to take basic Science courses, and her methodology of, "you either get it or you don't," was not compatible with my, "learn through instruction," approach to education.

I stayed for an extra two to three hours each evening,

sitting in her cramped office, along with two or three other students.

"I'm really trying. I don't understand a lot of this, but I am willing to learn." I told her.

"I can tell that you're trying." She said.

Good. At least she knew that I was making an effort. It was probably obvious by the fact that I was in her office just as much as she was, but I reminded her every so often just to make sure that she knew. A few more weeks passed and though it hadn't been that long, I felt like I had been in her class for years. I still didn't have a good grasp of most of what we were studying, but I put in more effort for that class than perhaps any that I have ever taken.

I had an appointment to speak with the Dean of Student Affairs for the school about what was happening, and they informed me that each professor is allowed to teach their class however they see fit. As long as the content is being taught, there isn't much that they can do. He did say that he would speak to the professor and see if perhaps she could make some of the assignments easier. As expected, this only made her angry at me for going above her head to try and get something done.

One day Student Support Service was giving out free pizzas in the lobby of the Science Building which was the building in which the professor's class was held. The other students in that class and I got a pizza and took it up to her classroom. She was elated at the gift, though a bit skeptical since we were all failing her class.

"Thank you. You're all still failing though." She reminded us.

None of us had expected that the pizza would improve our grades. It was just a small gesture to say that we were trying and respected her as our professor. A few days after that, someone in our class announced that they were finally passing with a low "C". We were all envious of them and I have to admit that I was more than a little frustrated. My effort did not seem to be paying off.

Two hours after class ended, I was still in the professor's office going over problems from earlier in the day.

"You see that I'm making an effort." I said.

She nodded and narrowed her eyes, "Yes."

"Can you guarantee me at least a "C" in your class if I continue to put in this amount of work?" I asked, thinking that I had just made a completely reasonable request.

"No. I won't promise you anything." She said.

My heart sank and I felt defeated. The official last day to drop the class was only a few days away and I hated the thought of not finishing. There were only about five of us left in the class by then and two of the other students who were studying with me that day heard the whole conversation. They went and dropped the class right after our study session.

That evening the stress was weighing on me. I had never failed a class in my entire life, what would happen if I failed this one? It wasn't even so much the idea of failing that bothered me, it was all of the wasted evenings of extra work that had led to no progress. I was trying harder than I ever had in a class and the professor didn't seem to care.

My breaths were coming in ragged gasps and I needed some fresh air. I felt like I couldn't fully fill my lungs with oxygen. I went outside and sat on my parent's porch swing. It had rained earlier in the day, so the swing was wet, but I didn't care. I sat down, soaking the bottoms of my pants, and tried to breathe.

I took in a deep breath of air and it still didn't feel like enough. I focused on my breathing for the next few minutes. My fingertips were tingling and beginning to go numb. The night air was cold against my skin and I knew that I shouldn't stay outside too long, or I would risk getting sick, but I had to fill my lungs with air…I had to.

Some time passed and I was able to get control of my breathing. When I went back inside the house, I talked to my parents about what was going on and they gave me the advice to drop the class. I had known all along that it might come down to that, but I was completely in denial.

"If it's causing you this much stress then it isn't worth it." They said.

The next day I went and dropped the class. That summer I took the online Physical Science class that was offered by the community and technical college and passed it with a very high "A". The content was not easy, but it was taught in a way that was relevant to educators. We learned how to apply specific concepts to lessons that we would be teaching in our own classrooms someday. If we had questions, the professor explained the answers in terms that made sense to us.

No matter what anyone says, there should not be that big of a difference in how classes are taught. It is one thing to have a professor that prefers specific methods, but to have the same class with such drastic differences in content and outcomes should not happen. If it ever does get to that point, I feel it is the college's or university's responsibility to investigate and determine why there is such a difference in student outcomes.

For the most part, professors tend to run their classes however they see fit. While the majority of professors are experts in their field, their goal should be to educate their students. When only two or three students make it to the end of your class, and even those are merely scraping by, you should consider a different profession. I have no doubt that my professor was a brilliant physicist, but there is a difference in being an expert in a field of study and knowing how to convey that knowledge to a classroom full of students.

Sometimes, you get lucky and a really good professor comes along. These are people who know what they are talking about, and who are able to pass on their knowledge to you in a way that is lasting. That particular professor was not alone in her behavior, as I have had many others that treat their classes with similar irreverence.

In another Science class that I took later on, I was given a zero for a daily grade. I received a phone call moments before class was to begin telling me that my car had been hit in the school parking lot. I told the professor and he said that he didn't care, if I missed his class then I would receive a zero for that day. The security office had requested that I stop by as soon as I could, so I took the zero and left to check on my car.

As an educator, I find it difficult to relate to those two professors. I have always tried to be understanding of the situations that my students face. Life is not easy and often times it is extremely difficult, but when you go to an educator seeking advice or even a bit of sympathy and all you get are dismissive grumblings, it can be all the more disheartening. I hope that nobody ever feels like they can't come to me with their problems, because it never hurts to care about what others might be going through.

I am still learning not to take things too seriously. There may come a day when I am able to completely let go of the stress in my life. The problems that I face now won't seem so big when I look back on them in a few years. Looking back on that Physical Science class, I can't believe that I wasted so much time and energy caring about something so insignificant. I had another option, though I refused to see it for the longest time, and in the end, I still earned my degree with honors. I have one piece of advice for you, no matter what you are going through at the moment...don't panic. The time you spend worrying, is time wasted.

46

THE WAIT

When I was younger, I would wonder what it would be like to be older. I think that is one of the saddest things about childhood. We spend so much time trying to grow up and be adults that by the time we realize we have become adults we want nothing more than to be like we were when we were children. So much of life seems to be spent waiting.

Waiting on your next birthday.
Waiting to be old enough to drive.
Waiting to graduate high school.
Waiting to finish college.
Waiting to get an interview for a job.
Waiting to find out if you got the job.
Waiting for a promotion.
Waiting for the next bill to arrive in the mail.
Waiting to pay off your car and house.

Waiting to retire.

Waiting to...

It is unfortunate that so much of our time is spent waiting on what is "supposed" to happen next. When things don't go our way, we think that perhaps we need to set new goals or try even harder than we did before because the goal is what is important. Right? We are told from the time that we are cognizant that we need to set goals, both short-term and long-term. I recall having an entire lesson on this in elementary school and even learning what "pipe dreams" were. Why is it that we put so much emphasis on the end goals? After all, the goal is what matters, isn't it?

However, when we finally reach our goals the first thing that we tend to do is set new ones. We start to work towards something else, whatever is to happen next. Even the "goal" is no longer what is important, but rather the "next" becomes the focus of our attention. It quickly becomes this sickening cycle that makes it impossible to rest and enjoy what we have accomplished because there is always something else to come.

It is only when we realize that the waiting is what matters, that we will be appreciative of our accomplishments. There is a song by Joshua Radin called *Streetlight* where there are a few lines that sum this concept up perfectly.

> *"I don't mind the wait it's fine*
> *As long as you know*
> *It's the wait that could be the something"*

When I hear those words, I am reminded to truly consider where I am at in life. Waiting is not a punishment, in fact the majority of good things that have happened in my life have happened during these times of waiting. The times in-between the major life events and goals are what I long for more than anything else. I try as much as I can not to stress over meeting goals and to just enjoy the little things. This is more difficult than one might think because we are trained from a young age to want to reach goals.

It's strange that we are told if we don't set goals then we are somehow doing something wrong. It is all a part of our competitive culture that celebrates achievement over simply being. The downside of this system is that enough is never enough. There is always one more goal to meet. It is like a perpetual Apple keynote, there is always just "one more thing."

Our goal should be to stop and recognize the moments that make up the in-between time. There is much more time spent between goals in our lives, and instead of seeing it as a negative, we need to see these moments as the part of life to truly enjoy. If we can do that then we will be able to get so much more out of the limited time that we are given.

47

SAME SKY

There are a few things that I have always been fascinated by, one of those things is the sky. When I was little, I would spend hours staring up at the clouds and trying to find shapes in them. Riding in the back seat of a car meant looking out the windows to try and derive meaning from the clouds.

As I grow up the sky takes on an entirely new meaning for me. Having been on flights, I have seen what the clouds look like from both above and below. I have looked down on them and seen that they are even more magnificent up close.

One concept that always steals my focus is that no matter where you are in the world, you will be standing beneath the same sky as everyone else. I could be a million miles away from my home, but if I were to look up at the sky and my family were to do the same, we would all be seeing the same sky. Of course, there are differences in appearance and weather, but I recognize the sky as one singular unit.

The sky holds so many things that are the same. Look up and you will see the same sun, the same stars, and the same moon as everyone else. While the sky holds undeniable truths for humanity, it highlights similarities and differences. The objects in the sky are the same, but how you perceive them might be entirely different. Depending on the night, the moon might look closer to the Earth. I have seen the moon while in Paris, and it looks close enough that you could reach out and touch it.

I cannot help but apply these concepts to other aspects of life. My mind has always wondered about similarities and differences. Does what I know to taste like strawberry taste the same to you? Is my color blue the same as yours? Others must think of these things to, or perhaps I am the only one? I don't think that I am.

One of my closest friends in high school would discuss things like this with me. We would choose a concept or topic and try to make sense of it through our words. We came up with a phrase that we would use with one another. When asked what we were doing, we would respond in a peculiar way that held meaning for us.

"What are you doing?" One of us would ask.

"Thinking thoughts that have previously been thought of." The other would respond.

Looking back on this I understand that these are concepts that most high school students would not want to bother themselves with. We had determined that there was the possibility that all thoughts have already been had by someone in the past. The order of them or the application of them may be different, but was there any chance that a truly original thought could be had anymore?

I often hear that there can never be another company like Apple or Amazon because for them to succeed in the way that they have, they had to create their companies at the exact times that they did. Just as those skeptics argue there could never be another Amazon, there can still be companies that mimic or mirror them, just in a different way. The application of a concept or idea is the only differentiating factor.

So, maybe I am telling you something that you already know. My words have almost definitely been use in a similar structure by someone in the past. The words themselves have been used an innumerable amount of times. However, the application of how I express these words and the intent behind them may be unique.

When you look up at the sky, take a moment to stop and allow yourself to wonder who else is looking at that same sky with you. It is a unifier of all life on this planet and something that we all share. There are many different things that this could be said of, but for me knowing that when I look up and see the wonders above, they are the same wonders that you can have from anywhere in the world.

48

NO SUCH THING AS LUCK

The things that I thought I wanted to accomplish when I was younger have already been done. It seemed like I needed to decide on a certain path that would help me to accomplish my goals, but what I have come to realize is that without meaning to, I have been able to accomplish all of the goals that I once imagined impossible. Things that I didn't foresee happening in my future happened so casually and with purpose that I didn't even realize it until I took a step back and examined my life.

Here is a list of some of the things that I always wanted but never saw happening for myself:

- Become an educator.
- Own a house near my family.
- Graduate college with zero student loans or debt.
- Own a chihuahua.

- Travel the world.
- Be financially stable.

All of the things listed above have happened for me. Most of them happened in such a way that I didn't realize it at first. Everyone's life is different, and I understand that some have it better or worse than I do. I have found that when I prioritize my faith and family, amazing things happen, and they do so without any announcements. Our blessings aren't always obvious. It is so easy to get caught up in life and forget to take count of the blessings we have been given.

There is a quote that I once read, and though I am unable to find the original source of the quote, it has stuck with me.

> "Remember that once you dreamed of being where you are now."

That quote is so true. When I was younger, I never would have dreamed that my life would be the way it is now. Some things went the way I would have thought that they would, while others definitely have not. Everything in life is not perfect, very few things ever are, but appreciating what you have been given is an excellent place to start.

Some might say that all of this has happened by luck, but I would disagree with that sentiment. I have worked hard to accomplish some things, while others have fallen into place. I put my trust in God and I truly believe that the things that have happened in my life have happened because he allowed them to. You can account for the things in your life by assuming they happen by chance, but I don't believe that. If we left our lives up to chance, then there would be much more chaos and destruction in the world. There is structure and meaning to everything.

Even scientist that denounce that there is a God admit that there is an underlying order to the universe. If chaos and chance are your only markers for how things happen then I think you would agree that the world would be an entirely different place than it is. From cell structure all the way down to a single atom, there has to be a perfect design for them to function. It has been my undeniable experience that there is no such thing as luck.

49

LEARNING TO FLY

One thing that I have always been afraid of has been heights. I remember the first time that this hit me. I was standing on the bank behind my parent's house and when I looked down, it wasn't more than ten feet off the ground, but I got a sick feeling in my stomach. Ever since then, just thinking about heights makes me break out in a sweat and feel sick.

There have been times in my life when this fear has kept me from doing things. If there is anything on a vacation that involves heights, I usually skip it. I even turned down going to the top of the Montparnasse tower that overlooks the city in Paris. If I had it to do over, I would go to the top of that tower and see what I would have been missing.

I have always loved traveling, but I knew that if I really wanted to go to places far away, I needed to be able to fly. I had the opportunity to go to France for a few days and it was going to be my first time flying...by myself. I was nervous and excited at the same time. I was worried that I would not do well on an airplane and the entire trip would be ruined by the stress of being so high off of the ground.

My first flight was from a smaller airport. The airplane was tiny compared to the one that would take me from the USA to France. When the plane took off from the ground, I felt sick to my stomach, this feeling got even worse when I looked ahead as we ascended higher into the sky. It appeared as if the plane was tilted at a seventy-degree angle.

I was sitting by the window, something that I wanted to do because I was determined to conquer this fear of mine. I couldn't let my fear of heights keep me from seeing the world. When the plane leveled, I looked out the window and saw that we were above the clouds. Everything below looked miniature. I was impressed by how different the world looks from the sky.

I had a thought as I sat there, realizing that only a thin piece of metal separated me from the outside. What could I do if something were to happen? The answer was nothing. If something were to happen to me at this altitude there would be little to nothing that I could do to save myself. It was this realization that brought me peace of mind. It was silly to worry about things like that when ultimately, I had no control over them.

When I accepted this fact, I felt much more at ease. I wanted to enjoy every second of my view. When the plane landed at Washington Dulles Airport, I was surprised at how much fun the experience of flying had been. It was scary at first, especially since I was flying alone and wouldn't be meeting the other educators on this trip until I arrived in Paris.

The airplane from Washington Dulles Airport to Paris, France was a long one that lasted around seven hours. I have since taken flights to France that have lasted longer than that, so the seven-hour flight wasn't so bad after all. There was a child sitting in the row beside me with their parents. The child cried for the majority of the flight.

I was in the middle row with a seat between me and the next person. It was nice because both of us used it to hold the wrappers and trays from the food that was served on the flight until the attendant came by to pick it up. Anyone that has ever flown knows that any small amount of extra space is valuable, especially on a flight lasting more than a few hours.

The announcements were in both English and French and this was the first time that I realized I was actually going to France. I have always dreamed of going there, ever since taking French classes in high school. It just seemed like one of those dreams that you have that never really comes true. The flight was smooth except for when we had one stint of turbulence that lasted about fifteen minutes.

I paid for the expensive Wi-Fi on the flight so that I could check-in with my parents and let them know that everything was going fine. The internet on these flights is horrendous and should really be free for no more than it provides you with. I spent around $30 and got about an hour of Wi-Fi.

I had been told by the company that booked my travel to try and sleep on the flight to Paris. I knew that I should, and I truly did want to, but I was just too excited. The seats are not extremely comfortable, nothing like the plush ones that recline in first class, so it was not as if I could sleep without trying to anyway. I was not tired, and I honestly didn't want to miss a moment of that experience. I wish that I was able to sleep on flights because I would be much more rested for touring after landing, but that isn't something that comes naturally to me.

When we landed, I exited the plane and went into the airport to be greeted by a massive sign on the wall that read, "Bienvenu" which means "Welcome". It was my first greeting in France! I spent about an hour going through the security checkpoint where they verify your passport and flight information one final time before allowing you official entrance into the country. These checkpoints always make me nervous even though when I travel, it is always for a legitimate reason. The atmosphere is usually tense and it makes even the innocent feel as if you are guilty.

Of course, I passed through without any problems. I had made it past the final step to being in Paris! The air feels and smells different in France. It is a scent that is distinct and easily recognizable, but that after a few minutes you start to lose. I can't tell you what it smells like, only that it smells like France. I have heard people say that Paris smells bad, but I don't think that is the case at all. New York smells bad, trust me, but Paris has a scent all its own and I think there is a very distinct difference in smelling bad and smelling different.

I had survived my first flights and actually enjoyed them. When the other teachers found out that it was my first time flying and that I had been by myself on an international flight, they were in shocked. I didn't find navigating the airports to be difficult, the system just made sense to me. I am glad that I did take the opportunity and not say "no" simply because I was afraid of heights. While I still have some issues when it comes to heights, I am just glad that they don't extend to flying. I actually love flying and look forward to the flights almost as much as the trips themselves.

On the return flights home, I went from Paris to Belgium and then from there back to Washington Dulles and then on to Roanoke, Virginia. On the flight from Belgium to Washington Dulles, I blacked out from exhaustion, so I don't recall anything aside from getting on the plane and waking up once to use the bathroom and eat. If you ever get the chance to fly somewhere, take it. We live once and I personally want to see the beauty of this planet from as many vantage points as possible.

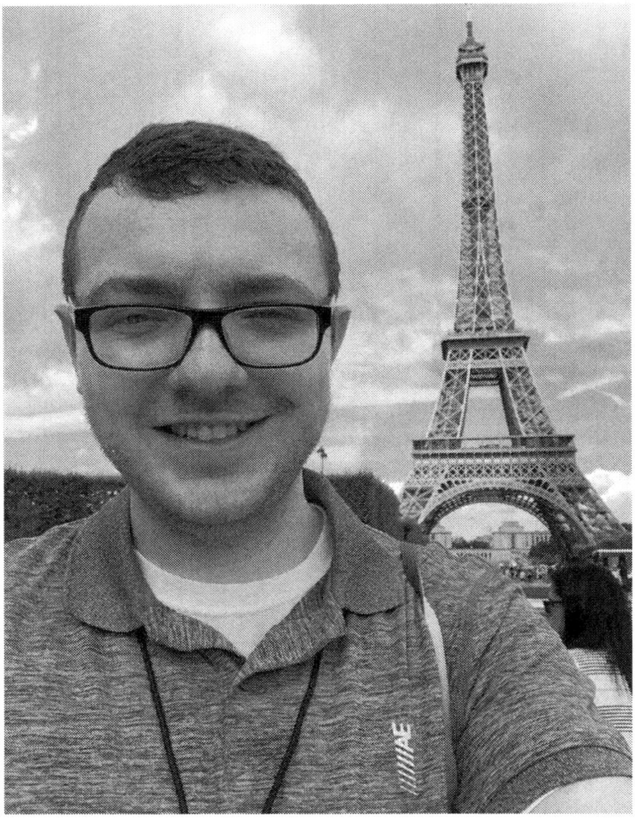

50

GROWING UP WEST VIRGINIA

Growing up in West Virginia is not at all like how it is portrayed on television and in books. If you were to go by the things that the media says about this state, then you would probably be afraid to visit. Something interesting that I have learned is that these stereotypes seem to be created and spread here in America.

On one of my trips to France, just about everyone that I met asked where I was from. When I told them West Virginia they almost always started to sing "Take Me Home, Country Roads" by John Denver. I learned that American culture is spread through media a lot in Europe. I was surprised to hear American music playing in shops throughout the country.

When I would explain that West Virginia is surrounded by mountains, the French seemed interested. They did not appear to have negative preconceived ideas about the state. What they knew about West Virginia came specifically from the song, and the song portrays the natural beauty of the state rather than the stereotypes.

Talking to a tour guide in Paris, explaining that I lived in a rural part of the United States, I could see and hear their longing to visit such a place. It was nice to be able to talk about West Virginia with people who didn't view it negatively just because of something they had heard. In the United States, rumors seem to spread and deter people from visiting.

Over the past few years, people have learned that the state is quite different from what they had imagined. The tourism industry has picked up quite a bit and houses and land are selling every day to visitors from out-of-state who come for a vacation and end up staying for a lifetime. Since I can't say for sure what you already know about the state, I will tell you what it was like for me growing up here.

Seeing mountains is an everyday occurrence. When visitors first see the mountains they are in awe. I could step out on the front porch of my parent's house and see peaks all around. I hope that I never take them for granted, but I know that I must because I see them so often. That is one of the cruxes of being human, after time we begin to ignore the beauty that we see the most in pursuit of whatever it is that we don't have.

While the mountains and their natural beauty are definitely a perk of living here, the people are probably the best part of the state. I have been fortunate enough to get to do some traveling to different parts of the United States and Europe, and I always notice a stark contrast in how people talk to one another. I am not talking about someone's accent, though West Virginian's tend to have a pretty recognizable one, but I am talking about the tone and manner that people use with one another.

In West Virginia the people tend to be friendly and open, even to strangers, but until I started traveling, I didn't realize that its different in other places. On a trip to visit my aunt and cousins in Pennsylvania, I had many encounters with people who were what I consider to be rude. I have been told repeatedly that people up North just have different personalities than further down South, but to me there is a difference in having a unique personality and talking down to someone.

In France, the people tend to be direct and to-the-point, but I don't consider that to be rude behavior. If I were to ask someone for directions in West Virginia I would probably end up knowing that person's life story by the time our conversation ended. In New York, someone would probably ignore me and shove me aside just for good measure. I understand that not everyone who lives up North is rude, in fact I have met some very nice people there, but the general atmosphere is much more tense than it is in West Virginia.

My aunt took me, my cousin Nathan, and my Nanny to New York for the day since I had always wanted to go. During that time my aunt and Nanny witnessed someone having their passport stolen and my aunt was yelled at for asking for help. We were on our way back home and trying to find our gate at Penn Station for the Amtrak. There were employees of the station all around wearing their uniforms, seemingly not very busy, so it should not have been a major deal when my aunt went up to one and asked how we were supposed to find our gate.

I have flown and been to some of the biggest international airports in both America and Europe, airports where very few people speak English, and I was able to navigate them without any problems. However, the way that Penn Station in New York City is set up is atrocious. I still don't think it was unreasonable for my aunt to ask an employee of the station for help.

The woman stopped walking and looked at my Aunt as if she might hit her.

"What?" The woman asked,

"We need help finding our gate. We know where the terminal is, but there isn't a gate listed."

The employee gritted her teeth together and narrowed her eyes, "I don't have time for this! Learn to read your ticket. There is NO gate until five minutes before boarding."

The woman didn't wait for my aunt to respond, she just walked off. This stranger just talked down to my aunt like she was a child and walked away as if this is how she treated everyone. I was in shock, but my aunt wasn't as visibly phased by it as I was. I suppose that living up North requires growing a thicker skin towards those types of things.

My aunt is an extremely caring person, so to see someone

talk to her that way was unexpected. The employee was indeed correct, the station did not announce which gate you had to be at until five minutes before boarding. To me, this made no sense because what ends up happening is everyone rushes the gates when they are announced and you are crammed through a tiny door with hundreds of other passengers, bodies pressed against one another in the hot, airless stairway that leads down to the tracks. It was not a pleasant experience being squashed by all of the other passengers as we descended the steps. There was an escalator, but of course it was broken; who knows how long it had been out of order.

Later, on that same trip, as my Nanny and I were at the Philadelphia Airport getting ready to board our flight, I had another unnecessarily rude encounter. Since we purchased the cheapest tickets available, we were not assigned seats until a few minutes before boarding. The attendant at the American Airlines counter asked us to bring her our tickets. My Nanny handed her ticket over and the attendant started typing on the computer. I laid my ticket on the counter so that she could get my information next. I was baffled by what proceeded to happen.

The attendant stopped what she was doing on the computer and looked at me, "Excuse me! You can hand me your ticket. You don't throw your ticket up here on the counter and expect that I'm just going to pick it up."

I smiled thinking that she must be joking. I had simply placed my ticket on the counter to save her the time and trouble of having to ask for it again. We were the only two passengers that she was "assisting" so I wasn't sure what the big deal could have been.

"Pick it up and hand it to me." She shouted.

I'm sure that everyone else in the airport was wondering what could possibly be going on. She was acting like I had just crumpled my ticket into a ball and thrown it at her. I find this type of behavior unnecessary and inappropriate. This goes beyond someone not liking their job; it stems from a general lack of respect for others.

I handed her my ticket and once we were assigned seat numbers we waited for boarding to begin.

"What was all of that about?" My Nanny asked me.

"Who knows?" I said, genuinely confused where the attendant's outburst had come from.

When boarding began, we waited for our ticket class to be called. The same attendant was standing at the entrance to the boarding area. She asked everyone the same question.

It was something along the lines of, "Do you have any electronics or batteries in your carry-on?"

I said, "No, I don't."

I followed the person in front of me, just as every single person before me had done, and I heard a shout coming from behind.

"Excuse me! Sir! When I ask you a question, you answer!"

It was that same attendant. I turned and lost my patience with her. I shouted back, "I told you, No. I don't have any batteries!"

She mumbled something to herself and turned back to the rest of the passengers waiting to board. Luckily, that was my worst experience at an airport and I assume that it is bound to happen eventually if you fly enough. When I mentioned the incident to American Airlines they just replied by saying that they provide excellent service so they weren't sure what I was talking about. Gee...I wonder where their employees get their attitudes?

So the people in West Virginia tend to have a much more relaxed approach to conversations. Life here moves at a much slower pace and I think more and more people are finding that desirable. I know a large portion of my community, not just a small circle of close friends, but I know the names and happenings of acquaintances and the people they know. Sometimes it can feel like people know a little too much about one another, but I find it preferable to nobody ever taking the time to get to know me.

I think that a lot of the differences in personality and public behavior can come from the lifestyle presented in a specific area. I get it, New York is fast-paced and could definitely be a stressful place to live. I mean, I was there for a day and my nerves were on edge. However, I cannot help but compare that experience to my experience in France. The behavior I experienced in New York and Philadelphia is what I consider to be rude and uncalled for, whereas in France I understood that a quick conversation was not to be rude but to be efficient.

As we boarded the airplane in Philadelphia and took our

seats, I did the only thing I thought would make a difference and I said a prayer for that attendant who had been rude to me. Not a prayer of malice, wanting God to punish her in some way for how she had behaved towards me, but a prayer that God would help her through whatever was bothering her and causing her to lash out at people. At the end of the day, I have the peace of mind that God is always watching out for me, and I understand that not everyone does. I hope that whatever was going on in her life was resolved and she saw that God helped her through it.

People's actions tend to be rooted in faith here in West Virginia and that is where so much of the caring and kindness comes from. People here will tell you what they believe, but they won't shun you for believing differently. West Virginia is a place where you can have faith in what you believe and not be looked down upon for it. I have only ever known West Virginia to be a welcoming place for strangers. This state is known for being home to some of the friendliest, most hard-working individuals in the country.

My experiences growing up in West Virginia have varied, but when it comes down to it, I love living somewhere that the rest of the fast-paced world has seemed to have forgotten. Those who do visit tend to discover this hidden gem of a state that has always been in plain sight. After all, West Virginia is a state that was formed because in 1865 it was determined that we did not support slavery and Virginia did, therefore we needed to become our own state.

No, we are not the Western part of Virginia. From the

start, West Virginia has been its own state in more ways than one. There are many elements that define the characteristics of the people and this place. We are our own state and I am proud to have grown up in such a magnificent area that is unlike anywhere else in the world.

51

OH, BROTHER

My brother, Andrew, and I have always been pretty close. He is only a year younger than I am, so I don't remember a time in life when he wasn't there. In all of my parent's old home videos we are both present. Luckily, they captured a lot of early memories that I can no longer recall, so that I can watch them anytime that I want. My parents took on the jobs of family history archivists shortly after I was born, so there are very few moments that were not documented in some form or another.

There is one home video that has become famous amongst our family members. I was only a few years old at the time. It is just a regular day and I am talking to the camera about who even knows what. A common thread between my families old home videos is me being heard talking about...basically everything. I always seemed to be talking when I was younger, and it didn't even seem to matter if I had anything important to say because I assumed that everything I said was important.

So, I'm giving a speech to the camera about whatever popped into my little head and all-of-the-sudden I turn and point to my brother who is sitting on the couch with his foot in his mouth.

"Bubby chewing his nails!" I shout.

My brother just stares into the camera with his toes in his mouth like he got caught doing something that he shouldn't have been doing. My parents have always tried to get my brother and I to stop chewing our fingernails, but my brother was somehow able to maneuver his leg so that he could reach his foot up to his mouth. Small moments like those have become iconic in my life's story.

When my brother started school, I was excited because he was only a year behind me. I imagined that I could tell him everything that he needed to know in order to be successful because I had already been through it myself. There were plenty of times when I told him which teachers to avoid or how to get good grades by playing to a teacher's preferences. However, he had his friends at school and I had mine. It wasn't the socializing experience that I had imagined where I would get to see him throughout the day. Schools tend to keep grade levels separated, so while I would see him on occasion I didn't see him often at school.

Any time that I won anything in class I would save it to bring home and give to my brother. If I won a piece of candy or a prize from a treasure box, I would save it and bring it home with me so that he could have it. Though nobody ever told me I had to, I have always felt like I am responsible for him in some ways and try my best to look out for my younger brother. I have had friends and known people who talk badly about their brothers or sisters, wanting the world to know how much they don't get along, and I feel bad for them because I know what they are missing out on. I am thankful that my brother and I have never felt that way towards one another.

One time when we were relatively young and in elementary school, we were play fighting and it got intense. I had slammed him on his back and knocked the air out of him. Fear immediately rushed through me because I was worried that I had seriously hurt him. The other reason that I was afraid is because I knew when he recovered and regained his breath I would have to pay for what I had done. I knew my brother would be getting me back for that.

Luckily, we have never really been competitive with one another, aside from in video games. We have a lot of different interests, and we share a few, so we have always had enough differences that being competitive didn't make sense. We were too different to compete with one another at the things that we were individually good at.

My brother was interested in playing sports, so he played basketball for the school and at the local recreation center any chance that he got. I played basketball for one year and hated it. I dreaded having to go to practices for a game that I wasn't that interested in. During that time my Dad was the assistant coach and our team was pretty horrible so luckily nobody took it too seriously.

In college, we ended up having one of the same Math classes. Neither of us are great at Math, in fact it is my least favorite subject. If I had to pick a favorite subject it would be English or anything technology related. In that Math class both of us struggled, but I was glad to be in there with him because I was able to help him out on occasion when he needed it. It wasn't my first college Math class, so I had a bit more experience than he did in dealing with college-level equations.

At the end of the day, I know that he will always be there for me when I need him, and I am positive that he knows the same about me.

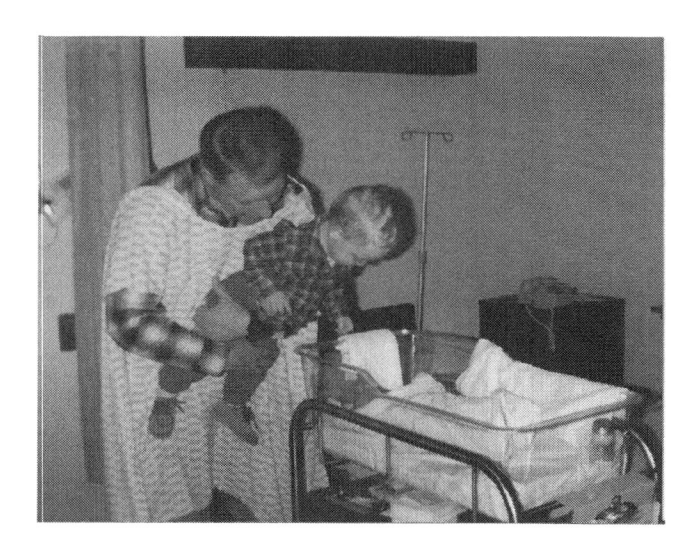

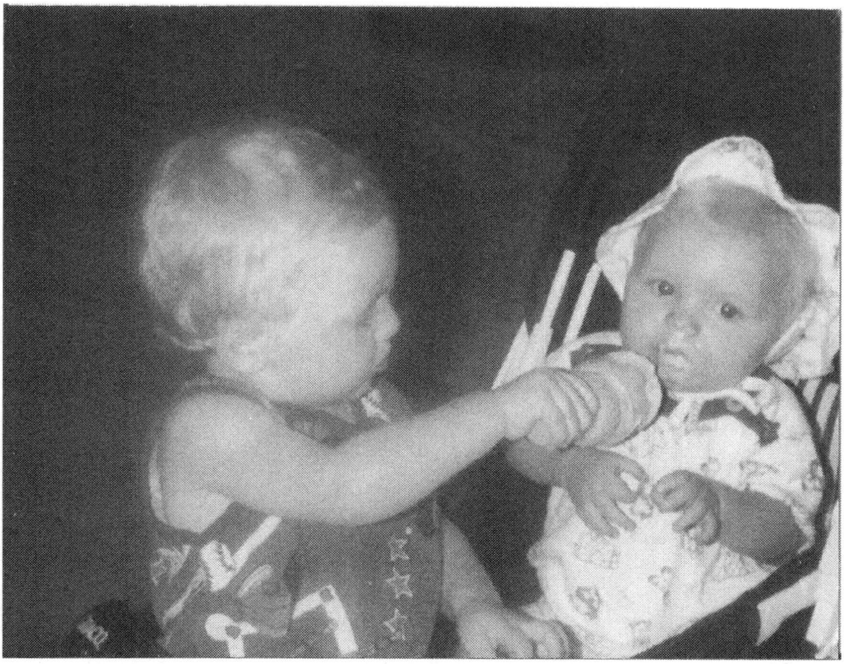

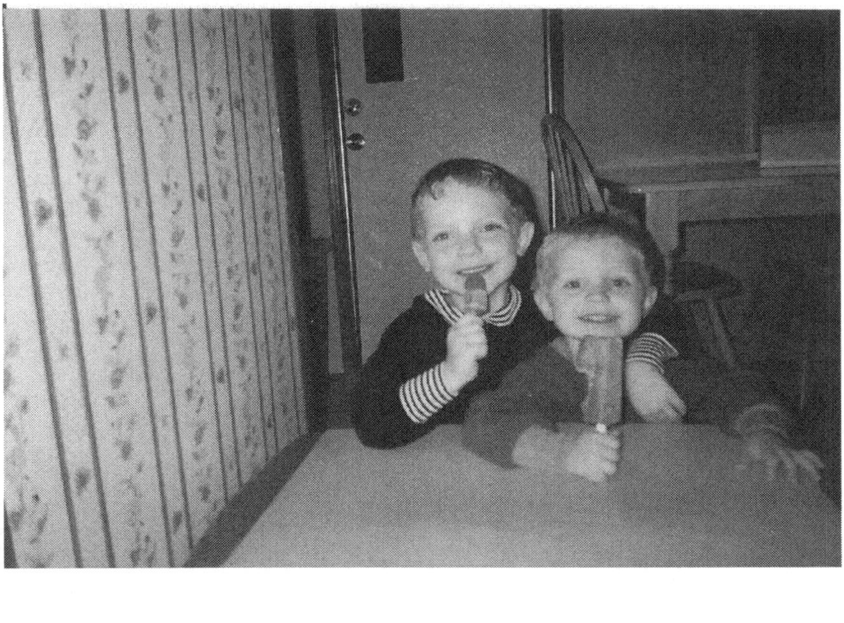

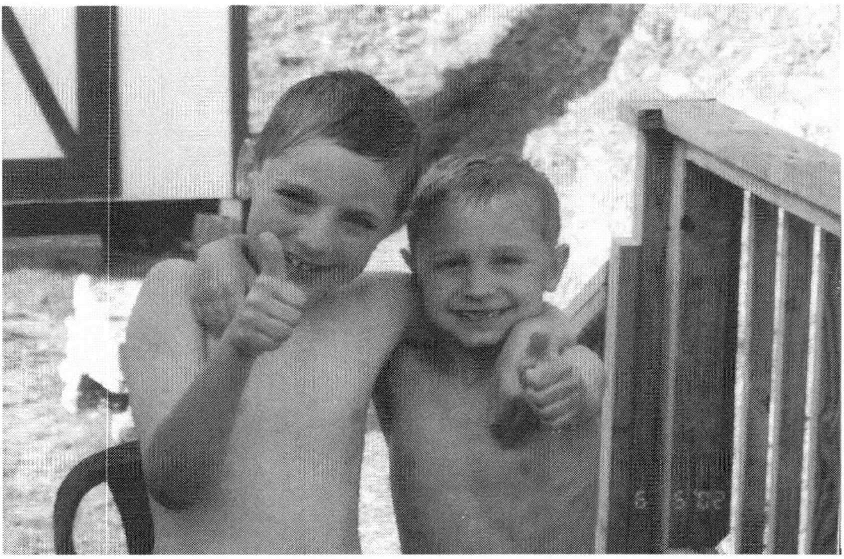

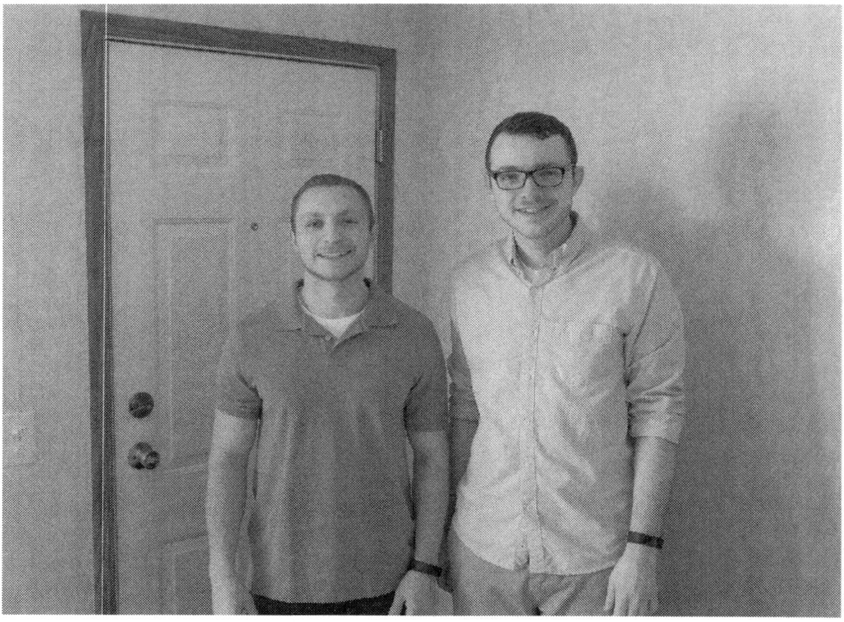

52

EVERYTHING

I have always had the problem of having too many interests. When I see people that have one hobby and they are extremely dedicated to it, I am envious of them. I can't just have one hobby or one thing that I really like. I tend to want to do everything at once. It gets to be exhausting because I also want to do my best at everything.

I love art, reading, writing, gaming, learning, teaching, traveling, spending time with my family, cooking, business, photography, making YouTube videos, and a million other things. Sometimes it gets to be overwhelming because I am also a perfectionist. I have been trying for a long time not to be a perfectionist and to be satisfied with things being just average, but I struggle with that.

To give you an example, you might think that reading is not a super competitive thing. Yet, somehow, I have made it one. I keep track of the books that I read and at the end of the year I try to meet the goal that I set for myself. This in itself isn't too bad, but each year I feel like I need to read more books than the year before. It doesn't always happen, but I still feel the pressure to read more.

If I am cooking then I don't want to just cook a simple meal, I want it to be the best looking and tasting meal that I could have possibly made. Baking a dessert usually ends up taking half the day or more because I won't be happy with the finished product unless it looks like it hopped off the screen of Food Network and landed on my kitchen counter. I strive for perfection and it has not been good for me.

I have been working to find the balance between perfection and enjoying whatever the finished product happens to be. I have had many health issues directly related to stress due to my insatiable desire to strive for perfection. It is exhausting and I wish I could learn to be happy with being average. I am sure that a lot of it has to do with my personality and the way that I revered school when I was younger, but as I grow older, I have come to realize that the only way to be everything at once is to not be perfect at any of it.

Perhaps if I could just choose one or two things that I wanted to focus on then I could strive for the pinnacle of excellence, but I don't want to do that. I don't want to just experience one or two things during my life. I want to experience as much of life as I can while I am here. I find so many things fascinating, I just need to learn how to accept that I will never be the absolute best at all of them.

If I can just succeed in the things that truly matter, then I will have been a success in my mind. If I can focus on faith and family, letting everything else be secondary, then that is really all that I need to do. Maybe you are like me and you feel like you are spreading yourself thin with all of your commitments and interests, if that is the case, then try what I am trying. Take a step back, decide what is absolutely necessary, and focus on those things while letting the rest simply be there waiting for when you have the time.

53

A MILLION DREAMS

My brother was the first one to move out of our parent's house. After college, I was able to live with them and save up the majority of my income. Had I not been able to do this then I never would have been able to afford to buy a house. I had spent a year living on campus during my time in college, but my brother forwent that experience and lived at home, going to the college that I eventually transferred to and graduated from myself.

Sometimes I wonder if having the money back that I had spent on room and board fees would have helped out much at all? I am sure that it would have, either that or I would have spent more money on useless things than I already did while in college. I find that when I have more money, I spend more money. This is something that I have been working on reconfiguring for years.

Somehow, I knew that my brother would be the first of us to move out for real. It wasn't that he hated living with our parents, neither of us did, but he wanted to experience the independence of living on his own. He found a place that he liked and though it was a fixer-upper he knew that he could rely on our family to help renovate it. I have to admit that when we were finished, it looked like an entirely new house. Up until then I had always questioned my brother's taste, but he made some really great decisions on the interior of the house.

I still had planned to live at home a few more years and save even more money to put towards a house. My plans changed when I learned that a house in his neighborhood was getting ready to go on the market. A family had inherited it and before they put it on the market, they asked my family if we knew anyone who would be interested. We looked at the house and I honestly thought that my parents were going to buy it because, aside from not having two full bathrooms, it seemed perfect for them.

They decided that they really wanted a place with two full bathrooms for when they have guests over, so they were going to pass on it. It was strange because I didn't feel like I was in love with the house, but I didn't not like it either. It just felt like somehow it was the right next step for me to take. I decided to make an offer that was quite a bit lower than what they were asking and somehow, I knew they would take it. I didn't question myself or feel overwhelmed by the decision like I had expected to, instead it just felt like something that I was supposed to do.

They accepted the offer and shortly after we began the renovation process on my house. I honestly could not have done the remodel without my family's help. The structure of the house was in good shape, aside from a few things that my Dad was able to fix, but there were a lot of little things that added up to months of work. For example, I took down the mirror from the wall in the half-bathroom and there was a hole the size of a basketball behind it.

You can expect little surprises like that when you buy a house. Luckily, there had only ever been one family to live there before I bought it. I like very simple and modern designs so that was the route that I took with my house. To me, simple is better. Too many decorations and colors are overwhelming and while they might look good in pictures, I wanted a place that I would be comfortable and relaxed living in.

It's really neat how a person's house tends to reflect elements of their personality. I have been in homes that are the perfect amount of lived-in so that they seem cozy, while mine tends to be very neat and orderly. I think that these preferences also spill over into other areas of our lives. I once had a student tell me that I had the neatest desk out of any teacher in the school. They were referring to the fact that I don't keep clutter on my desk, only the essentials. For me, having an organized workspace has always been key to me performing the best at my job.

Throughout the remodeling process, my Dad would play music through his phone to a Bluetooth speaker. My family had recently watched and fallen in love with the movie "The Greatest Showman", so that soundtrack became the soundtrack of the remodel. It was pretty much on repeat every evening that we worked. If my neighbors were able to hear anything between the loud noises of power tools and appliances being loaded and unloaded, then it would have been us singing alongside Hugh Jackman, Keala Settle, and the rest of the cast of the movie.

Something about that choice in music also felt right. The storyline of the movie focused on working hard and making impossible dreams come true. At the end of the movie there is just a simple scene that alludes to the idea that P.T. Barnum had everything he needed from the start. At that point in my life, I felt the exact same way.

For years, I had stressed over school, trying to get the correct education that would lead to a successful career, but without even trying, it was like all of that went away. Everything that was happening seemed to happen because it was supposed to. There are times in life when you feel like you are exactly where you are meant to be and that was one of them.

My life is not perfect, regardless of what some people believe. I have many struggles and faults of my own, but I try my best to focus on the good things. There are a million negative things that any one of us could choose to focus on each day, but as for me I would rather focus on a million dreams.

54

SUPPORT

When I hear the word "support" nowadays I think in terms of tech support. We hear the word so often that it almost starts to lose its meaning. To support something can mean a number of things. Growing up, I never really thought about the word, but I clearly understood it. There were those who had support for the things that they did and those who did not have support.

You can think of supporting someone in monetary terms or you can think of it the way that I do, and that is to be there for someone when they need you. I have always known that no matter what crazy idea I come up with, my family would be there to support me through it. Knowing that someone is always there for you, no matter what, is worth more than any amount of money.

It does not take an entire group of people to support

someone to be successful either. Having the support of a single person can make a world of difference. Read the biographies and memoirs of famous people and you will find that almost always, somewhere along the line, they had the support of someone. None of us can succeed on our own.

Think about the people in your life that have supported you and helped you to become the person that you are today. I hope that at least one person comes to mind. Now think about someone that you could support. Again, I hope that at least one person comes to mind. When I think back on the stories in this book, I realize more than ever that I didn't get to where I am on my own. Reflect back on memories from your own life and you will find that what I say is true. We all need the support of someone, and perhaps someone is waiting on you to be their support.

55

I NOW KNOW EVERYTHING

When I was younger you could ask me anything and I would look at you with a serious expression and nod my head.

"I know ehh-bee-stang." I would say matter-of-factly.

In my mind there was no question that I could not answer. Did I actually know the answer to every question? Of course not. The point was that to me there was nothing that I couldn't try to explain, no matter how little sense it made.

Growing into an adult is no easy task and everyone who has ever done it has truly accomplished something special. The older I seemed to get, the less confident I was that I actually knew anything. Sitting down and reflecting on my life thus far has been a journey that I wasn't sure I would be able to successfully take.

I have no problem dreaming up fictional worlds where reality is left behind, but deciding to write a book about the stories of my life was a difficult decision for me to make. When I look back at photos of the kid who would confidently answer any question given to him, I feel like I am looking at a different person. In many ways that is true.

In life, we experience ups and downs that test just how much we can handle. It has become obvious to me that having others to go through life with and support my decisions has been the deciding factor in how far I can make it. I want to surround myself with the people that will make more memories possible, truly special memories that I will be able to cherish for eternity.

As we grow, we learn, and as we learn we hopefully begin to understand. There is still much that I hope to understand, and it will be a lifelong process that I look forward to. Over the years, it is not that I knew less and less, it was that other things in life sometimes got in the way and clouded my vision. I realize that I had it figured out from the start. Right now, I am confident that I know the important things in life: faith, family, friends, and the moments we share.

In knowing that, I now know everything.

ABOUT THE AUTHOR

James Agee Jr. is the author of multiple young adult and children's novels. He resides in his home state of West Virginia where the surrounding mountains provide limitless inspiration. When he is not writing a book, he can be found reading one.

Many of his novels are inspired by actual true events, however as of date they are all purely works of fiction. His books offer a variety of stories so that all readers are able to find one of his works that they can enjoy.

Made in the USA
Columbia, SC
15 October 2021